GW00670240

the South West

FROM DAWN TILL DUSK

Leave it as it is. You cannot improve on it; not a bit.

The ages have been at work on it, and man can only mar it.

Theodore Roosevelt on the natural environment

the South West

FROM DAWN TILL DUSK ROB OLVER

TUART
HOUSE

STAPLES

I dedicate this book to my parents, Des and Pat, who first introduced me to the wild, open spaces.

The Charles and Joy Staples South West Region Publications Fund was established in 1984 on the basis of a generous donation to The University of Western Australia by Charles and Joy Staples.

The purpose of the Fund was to make the results of research on the South West region of Western Australia widely available so as to assist the people of the South West region and those in government and private organizations concerned with South West projects to appreciate the needs and possibilities of the region in the widest possible historical perspective.

The Fund is administered by a committee whose aims are to make possible the publication (either by full or part funding), by University of Western Australia Press, of research in any discipline relevant to the South West region.

First published in 2002 by
University of Western Australia Press
Crawley, Western Australia 6009
www.uwapress.uwa.edu.au
under the Tuart House imprint in association with the
Charles and Joy Staples South West Region Publications Fund
Reprinted 2002

This book is copyright. Apart from any fair dealing for the purpose of private study, research, criticism or review, as permitted under the Copyright Act 1968, no part may be reproduced by any process without written permission. Enquiries should be made to the publisher.

Copyright © Rob Olver 2002

National Library of Australia Cataloguing-in-Publication entry:

Olver, Rob (Robert), 1968– .
    The South West: from dawn till dusk.
    ISBN 1 876268 84 0.
    ISBN 1 876268 85 9 (pbk.).
    1. South-West (W.A.)–Description and travel. I. Title.

919.412

Front cover: (left to right): Surfer near Cape Naturaliste; Western grey kangaroo in Stirling Range heathland; Queen of Sheba orchid; Pineapple bush; Beedelup Falls near Pemberton.
Back cover: Merino sheep, Blackwood River Valley.
Endpaper: A golden sunset over Mondurup Peak from Talyuberlup, Stirling Range.
Page 2: A beautiful sunset at Contos Beach.
Pages 6–7: The magnificently wild and rugged Salmon Beach at Point D'Entrecasteaux.

Produced by Benchmark Publications, Melbourne
Consultant editor Amanda Curtin, Curtin Communications, Perth
Designed by Guy Mirabella, Melbourne
Maps by Country Cartographics, Ocean Grove, Victoria
Typeset in 11pt Joanna by Lasertype, Perth
Printed by Brown Prior Anderson, Melbourne

CONTENTS

ACKNOWLEDGMENTS
AND PHOTOGRAPHIC NOTES

I would like to thank: my friends Steve, Tony, Stuart, Colleen, Chris, Diane, Nigel and Lynnette, who have joined me on trips 'down south'; Maria Duthie and Tiffany Aberin, from the Department of Conservation and Land Management; Liam Kinsella, Ngilgi Cave, Yallingup; Simone Furlong, Leeuwin Estate; Nadia Harvey, Wise Winery; Tanya McCann and Cary Nuku, Caves Caravan Park, Yallingup; Trevor and Irene Collins, Bridgetown Caravan Park; Tony and Ayleen Sands, Pleun and Hennie Hitzert, Fred Butt and Dawn Dodds, from the Stirlings; Ann Burchell, Les and Angela Sharpe, Peter and Maleeya Form, Shelley Coad, Peter Thorn, Geoff Clarke and Campbell McCready, from the Porongurups; David O'Malley, Southern Regional Tourism Association.

The photographs in this book were taken with a Nikon F70 camera, using mainly Fuji velvia and sensia transparency film. I use a variety of lenses and polarizing and skylight filters to protect the lens and to improve colour saturation in bright or hazy conditions. Most photographs were taken using a tripod, which helps greatly to improve picture sharpness and quality.

ROB OLVER

PREFACE

The South West occupies a special place in my heart. I have become so attached to the forests, the hills and the coast of this region that it is now a part of my soul. This was not always the case. My first impressions when I arrived from South Africa, aged 16, were of a monotonous grey-green, flat land with windswept vegetation. The colours appeared muted compared to the subtropical vegetation I was used to, and there seemed little in the way of dramatic scenery. This view soon changed as I began, with my family, to explore our new home. Slowly the subtle beauty infiltrated my consciousness as I swam in the cool, clear waters of the southern beaches and climbed mountains in the Stirling Range. The sheer diversity of the landscape and the many shades and textures grew on me irresistibly. The urge to explore and discover more secrets of the South West has continually drawn me 'down south' on new adventures.

Even now, I have only scratched the surface of what the South West has to offer. I have yet to walk the full distance of the Bibbulmun Track; I have not seen large stretches of wilderness coastline; and there are so many photographs out there, waiting to be taken! This book is an attempt on my part to capture the moods, the sublime beauty and the soul of the South West. Undoubtedly, I have only partially achieved this, but I hope to inspire you to experience this magnificent area for yourself.

ROB OLVER

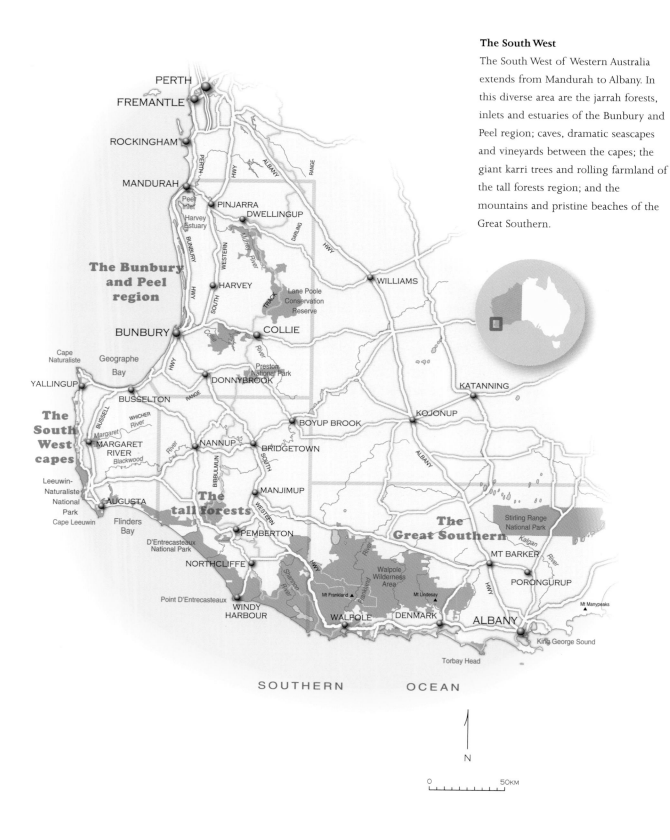

The South West

The South West of Western Australia extends from Mandurah to Albany. In this diverse area are the jarrah forests, inlets and estuaries of the Bunbury and Peel region; caves, dramatic seascapes and vineyards between the capes; the giant karri trees and rolling farmland of the tall forests region; and the mountains and pristine beaches of the Great Southern.

PERTH
FREMANTLE
ROCKINGHAM
MANDURAH
Peel Inlet
PINJARRA
DWELLINGUP
Harvey Estuary
PERTH HWY
ALBANY
RANGE
BUNBURY HWY
WESTERN HWY
Murray River
HARVEY
Lane Poole Conservation Reserve
DARLING HWY
WILLIAMS
The Bunbury and Peel region
SOUTH HWY
COLLIE TRACK
Collie River
BUNBURY
Cape Naturaliste
Geographe Bay
YALLINGUP
Preston National Park
DONNYBROOK
HWY
KATANNING
RANGE
BUSSELTON
WHICHER River
KOJONUP
The South West capes
BUSSELL
Margaret River
BOYUP BROOK
MARGARET RIVER
Blackwood
NANNUP
BRIDGETOWN
SOUTH
ALBANY
Leeuwin-Naturaliste National Park
River
BIBBULMUN
Cape Leeuwin
AUGUSTA
Flinders Bay
The tall forests
MANJIMUP
WESTERN
D'Entrecasteaux National Park
Stirling Range National Park
Kalgan
NORTHCLIFFE
PEMBERTON
Shannon River
HWY
Frankland River
The Great Southern
MT BARKER
River
PORONGURUP
Point D'Entrecasteaux
Mt Frankland ▲
Walpole Wilderness Area
Mt Lindesay ▲
HWY
Mt Manypeaks
WINDY HARBOUR
WALPOLE
DENMARK
ALBANY
King George Sound
Torbay Head

SOUTHERN   OCEAN

N

0   50KM

INTRODUCTION

The South West of Western Australia is an awe-inspiring place. This comparatively small area from Mandurah to Albany boasts some of the finest beaches in the world, along with stately jarrah and karri eucalypt forests, mountain ranges, a huge diversity of wildflowers and plant species, and many unique animal species. There are world-renowned wineries, limestone caves and historic towns. It is a visual feast—even seasoned travellers are often surprised by the unusual and beautiful natural landscapes to be found here.

The region's history starts with the arrival of Aboriginal people perhaps 40,000 years ago. The people here are of the Nyoongar language group, although separate tribes occupied different areas of the South West— for example, the Bibelmen near Northcliffe, the Mineng near Albany and the Binjareb around the Murray River. The tribal areas defined the hunting and gathering rights of each group, and customs were similar among Nyoongar people of the South West. Within the tribal territories, the population was made up of family clans, who travelled around following the seasonal supply of food. Each family had its home country, which was known as its 'karlup', or 'the place of my family fire'.

Karl, or fire, was very important to South West Aborigines, who used it for cooking, weapon and tool production, warmth and light, as well as for modifying the country around them. They would regularly set alight sections of their country, to promote the fresh growth of grasses, which attracted kangaroos, and to keep the forests clear and free of undergrowth. These fires were a useful hunting tool, flushing game out into the open where they could be speared. Although the Aboriginal population of the South West was probably less than 10,000 before the arrival of Europeans, the country was considerably changed by their presence. Many early explorers commented on the open and park-like nature of the land, due to Aboriginal fires, and there were tracks criss-crossing the countryside that were used by Aborigines for travel and trade with other groups.

Nyoongar people recognized six seasons in a year, based on the prevailing weather conditions. As hunters and gatherers, they utilized a great many of the plants and animals of the South West. They ate fruits, bulbs and tubers such as the wild pear (*Persoonia* sp.) and native potato (*Platysace cirrosa*). The roots of the Christmas tree (*Nuytsia floribunda*) and quandongs (*Santalam acuminatum*) were favoured foods, and even the highly toxic fruits of the zamia (*Macrozamia riedlei*) were eaten. Aborigines removed the toxins by burying the fruits for some time, then soaking them in water and finally roasting them on a fire. Balga (*Xanthorrhoea preissii*) was almost sacred to the Aborigines because it had so many uses. The flower spike was placed in water to

LEFT Southern cross (*Xanthosia rotundifolia*), Mt Lindesay.
OPPOSITE Late afternoon view of the historic town of Albany from Mt Melville.

produce a honey-sweet beverage called '*mungitch*', the leaves were used as thatch and bedding, and the trunks harboured witchetty grubs and contained a strong resin for making tools and weapons.

Nyoongars were expert hunters, eating anything from freshwater tortoises, fish and marron (delicious freshwater crayfish), to kangaroos, possums, goannas and emus. Their main weapons were spears (*keit* or *gidgee*), throwing sticks (*meara*), stone knives (*taap*), stone axes (*kodj*) and a non-returning boomerang called a '*curl*'. Aboriginal society was ordered, with complex social rules. There were, for example, two skin groups in the South West, and people from the same skin group could not marry. If these rules were broken, the punishment was severe, with offenders being forced to leave the tribe, speared through the thigh or occasionally even killed. Warfare between tribal groups was common, often sparked by revenge

killings on the death of a tribal member. In battle, two lines of warriors would stand opposite each other and hurl their *gidgees* or *meara* at the other side. Often without moving their feet, they would duck and weave to avoid what was thrown at them, and the battle usually ended when first blood was drawn on either side. Nyoongars lived well on the relatively rich lands of the South West and had plenty of time to develop a highly advanced oral tradition of songs and legends about the country they inhabited. These are known as the Dreamtime stories, many of which describe the creation of the land by giant mythological creatures such as the Waugal, or rainbow serpent.

The Aborigines must have been very surprised when tall ships appeared on the western horizon and landed on their shores. They initially welcomed the strangers, convinced that they were *djanga*, or the

returning spirits of Nyoongar dead, from an island to the west where the spirits rested. The first visits from European people were fleeting, but by 1830 two British settlements had been established, at Albany and Perth. Europeans slowly spread throughout the South West, changing the Aborigines' traditional way of life forever. At first, relations were amicable, with Aborigines showing settlers their water sources and best land, and being repaid with gifts of food and goods like axes and blankets. Nyoongars, however, did not understand the Europeans' concept of ownership of land and livestock, and this brought the two cultures into inevitable conflict. They climbed fences, wandered into houses to take food, and speared sheep and cattle, which had trampled their waterholes and reduced the numbers of indigenous game like kangaroos and possums. The response from the

Europeans was to imprison those responsible, and reprisals from Aboriginal people led to swift and deadly action from the settlers. There were deaths on both sides, but by far the majority were Aboriginal. These conflicts, along with the introduction of epidemic diseases like influenza and measles, had a devastating effect on the Aboriginal population, with high mortality rates and a relatively rapid breakdown of their society.

In the second half of the nineteenth century, many Nyoongars found employment on European farms in the South West as stockmen, labourers and domestic servants, and helped greatly in opening up this wild land. However, with the advent of the mission system in 1905, most were relocated to large towns. The 1905 Aborigines Act introduced many racist laws, including a curfew that prevented Aborigines staying in town centres after 6.00 p.m.

ABOVE The dolerite and granite
igneous cliffs of West Cape Howe, near
the southernmost point in Western
Australia, Torbay Head.
OPPOSITE Big old growth jarrah and
marri trees in Preston National Park.

and a prohibition on their drinking alcohol unless they had been granted 'citizenship rights'; most Aborigines were not citizens of their own country under the law at that time and had to apply for special permission to acquire these rights. From 1905 to 1963, the Chief Protector of Aborigines was the legal guardian of all 'mixed-race' children, and many were removed from their natural parents. During this period, the official policy was to 'assimilate' Aboriginal people into European society, and maintenance of their culture was actively discouraged. For example, children were forbidden to speak Nyoongar in schools, and it almost died out as a spoken language. Most Aborigines did not receive the right to vote until 1962 or full citizenship rights until 1967. Today Aborigines have started to reclaim their culture and reassert their rights in the land of their ancestors, but much work of goodwill on both sides will be necessary before reconciliation is possible.

The Dutch were the first European visitors to the South West. In 1622, the ship *Leeuwin* sighted a rocky cape that today bears its name, and the wild and lonely coast was called ''t Land van de Leeuwin', or 'the Land of the Lioness'. The Dutch had stumbled on Western Australian shores before, with Dirk Hartog landing on a remote island in the North West in 1616. The Dutch East India Company, searching for a quicker route to the spice islands, had recommended that ships sail due east from the Cape of Good Hope, using the prevailing westerly 'trade winds', before travelling north to Batavia (Jakarta). Many ships were blown further east than intended while following this route, ending up within sight of the Western Australian coast. The Dutch called this strange south land 'New Holland' but considered the country to be barren and useless. A number of their ships, including the *Batavia* in 1629 and the *Vergulde Draeck* in 1656, were wrecked on this dangerous coast.

In January 1627, the Dutch ship *Gulden Zeepaardt* (Golden Sea Horse), captained by Francois Thijssen and carrying Pieter Nuyts, encountered the south coast of New Holland. This vessel explored the Nuyts Archipelago in South Australia and travelled west along the southern coastline, eventually rounding Cape Leeuwin. Other Dutch ships like the *Grootenbroek* (1630) and *Emerloort* (1658) also skirted these shores. When the *Elburgh* arrived in 1658, Captain Jacob Pietresz Peareboom and others went ashore, possibly near Koombana Bay in Bunbury. However, for almost 150 years after, there was no exploration of note in the South West, and the Dutch never seriously considered settling in New Holland.

Eventually, the French and English began to take an interest in this land, mainly to thwart each other's colonial ambitions. In September 1791, the Englishman George Vancouver, in the sloops *Discovery* and *Chatham*, explored and named King George Sound and many other features like Point Possession, Princess Royal Harbour and Eclipse Island. He took formal possession of the southern coastline in the name of King George III. The land was deserted when he arrived, as the Aborigines were wintering in the interior, but Vancouver left behind gifts of beads, knives and looking glasses in their vacant huts, which must have a provided a great surprise for the Mineng when they returned. In December 1791, Rear-Admiral D'Entrecasteaux of the French Navy, with the ships *Recherche* and *Esperance*, sighted the south coast near a headland that was given the name Point D'Entrecasteaux. He continued east along the coast, suffering rough weather and storms around King George Sound, and eventually found shelter in Esperance Bay.

The French were back again in 1801, this time in the ships *Geographe* and *Naturaliste*, under the command of Captain Nicolas Baudin. With the expedition including a large number of scientists—botanists, zoologists, astronomers and geologists—the study of this new land finally began in earnest. Baudin arrived at Cape Leeuwin in May, and headed north around Cape Naturaliste into Geographe Bay. A number of visits to the shore were made, including a landing at Eagle Bay, but the expedition ran into difficulties and eventually a seaman, Timothy Vasse, was drowned trying to rescue equipment from a grounded longboat. A river was named after him, near the present-day town of Busselton.

In December 1801, Matthew Flinders sailed past Cape Leeuwin into Flinders Bay aboard the *Investigator*. He continued east to King George Sound, staying there for nearly four weeks and making friendly contact with the local Aborigines. On the day of departure he wrote:

> our friends, the natives, continued to visit us; and the old man, with several others being at the tents this morning, I ordered the party of marines on shore to be exercised in their presence. The red coats and white crossed belts were greatly admired, having some resemblance to their own manner of ornamenting themselves…but when they saw these beautiful red and white men, with their bright muskets, drawn up in a line, they absolutely screamed with delight…The old man placed himself at the end of the rank, with a short staff in his hand, which he shouldered, presented, grounded, as did the marines their muskets, without, I believe, knowing what he did.*

Flinders then continued his epic voyage around Australia.

Baudin conducted a second expedition to the south-west coast in 1803, visiting King George Sound. A few more explorers passed through, the last one of note being the Frenchman Dumont d'Urville, who sought shelter from storms in King George

* Quoted in D. Sellick, *First Impressions Albany 1791–1801: Traveller's Tales*, Western Australian Museum, Perth, 1997.

TOP The beautiful red flowering gum (*Corymbia ficifolia*), found naturally only in a small area near Walpole.
CENTRE A quenda, or southern brown bandicoot, next to the author's tent at Honeymoon Pool, near Collie.
BOTTOM A western bearded dragon, spotted in the Leeuwin-Naturaliste National Park.

ABOVE TOP *Hovea pungens* (devils pins), Darling Range.
ABOVE The nocturnal tawny frogmouth, common in the South West, is seen here in the Boranup forest near Margaret River.

The stately great egret, spotted in the Vasse-Wonnerup wetlands near Busselton.

Sound in October 1826. Whaling and sealing boats also plied the waters of the south coast at this time, and their rough captains and crew were responsible for the abduction of Aboriginal women, and other crimes.

Finally, the British decided to establish a colony in the South West, mainly to forestall any possible annexation by France of the western third of Australia. The first settlement in Western Australia was a convict outpost of New South Wales established at King George Sound in December 1826 by Major Edmund Lockyer. In 1829, a free settlement was founded in Perth, with the Swan River Colony being proclaimed on 18 June 1829. The amount of good agricultural land around Perth was limited, and it was not long before further settlements were estab-

lished in the South West. The first was at Augusta in May 1830, but most of these pioneers had relocated to the more hospitable country of the Vasse (around Busselton) by 1834. The Mandurah area was settled late in 1830 by Thomas Peel and his followers, while Bunbury was founded in 1841.

The colony started to grow, although development was so slow in the first two decades that the struggling colonists requested that convicts be sent from Britain to fill the desperate labour shortage. By this time, the eastern colonies of Australia had ceased taking convicts, and the British Government was anxious to find a new destination for its prisoners. The first boatload arrived in the Swan River Colony in 1850 and these men were put to work building public roads and buildings. The British Government

Magnificent karri forest in Boorara National Park, near Lane Poole Falls.

also greatly increased its expenditure on the colony, to maintain these convicts and their military guard.

The gold rushes at Kalgoorlie in the 1890s were the greatest spur to development of the region. The mines provided much-needed revenue, allowing the colonial government to construct railways and increase its spending on agricultural development. The population of Western Australia between 1892 and 1902 increased four-fold. At first the South West was not directly affected, but the increasing demand for fresh produce and other commodities like timber soon aided the growth and development of the area.

Between 1914 and 1918, many men and women from the South West became involved in World War I. About 32,000 soldiers from all over Western Australia were sent abroad with the Australian Imperial Force, including members of the 10th Light Horse regiment. Of these, 6,000 were killed in action and 16,000 were wounded in this terrible conflict. In the 1920s, the government put in place a number of Group Settlement Schemes at Margaret River, Manjimup and Denmark. Migrant workers from Britain and the city, many without any farming knowledge, were sent to areas of virgin bush, which they then attempted to clear and farm. These schemes were unsuccessful in the long term, and the advent of low wheat and wool prices in the Great Depression of the 1930s forced many families off the land. After World War II, returned servicemen were encouraged and helped financially to resettle in some of these areas. In these postwar years, Australia embarked on an ambitious immigration scheme to raise the country's population, and also accepted many refugees from wartorn Europe. Most of these immigrants, mainly from Britain, Ireland, Italy, the Netherlands and Germany, settled in the city but some went to the South West. Towns like Harvey and Manjimup still have large Italian communities.

Today the South West has a strong economy and supports a population of around 250,000 people. Traditional primary industries such as agriculture, forestry, fishing and mining are still of major importance, although this is changing gradually. Recently a few secondary industries, such as furniture manufacturing, and alumina refining at Pinjarra and Wagerup, have been developed.

The greatest growth industry in the region is tourism. Many thousands of visitors every year, drawn from all over Australia and overseas, come to enjoy the magnificent forests, hills and beaches, and to discover the unique plants and animals of this relatively pristine and unpolluted part of the world. Ecotourism is important in the South West. Tourists visit relatively new attractions like the Tree Top Walk near Walpole, as well as experiencing the 950 kilometre long Bibbulmun Track between Perth and Albany (see map, page 10). There are also plans for a mountain bike trail between Mundaring and Albany. This 850 kilometre trail, to be called the Munda Biddi Bike Trail, is scheduled for completion by October 2003. A related growth industry is viticulture, with expanding winery regions like Margaret River, Pemberton, the Great Southern and the Blackwood River valley. Tourism also helps to support a flourishing arts and crafts industry.

The South West is, in geological terms, a very ancient land indeed. There are no recently formed mountains or other landforms other than the Stirling Range, which was probably uplifted within the last 100 million years. Otherwise this part of Western Australia is relatively flat. The main physical feature is the Darling Scarp, which extends from north of Perth to beyond Nannup. The scarp is actually the edge of an ancient Precambrian plateau called the Western Shield, composed here of granite, gneisses and quartzite some 2,500 million years old. This gently undulating plateau extends over much of Western Australia. In the South West, parts of it have undergone laterization and contain deposits of bauxite, resulting from a period of high rainfall between 30 and 60 million years ago that deeply weathered and stripped the Precambrian rocks of nutrients. Today the Darling Scarp is extensively covered by jarrah, marri and karri forests, and is an important area for minerals such as bauxite, tin, tantalum and coal.

The Darling Scarp is the result of a north–south running fault line that extends from Exmouth in the north to Windy Harbour on the south coast. The land to the west of the fault, the Perth Basin, has been

displaced downwards about 10,000 metres over the last 400 million years. The Perth Basin has through the ages been filled with sediments of glacial and marine origin, with the superficial layers now reworked to form the sand dunes of the Swan Coastal Plain. Wetlands rich in wildlife are found between these ancient dunes where the watertable reaches the surface. The Swan Coastal Plain extends south until it meets the Leeuwin-Naturaliste Ridge near Dunsborough. This ridge is composed of hard, ancient granites overlain with limestone, and was formed by uplift between two parallel north–south trending fault lines. Two further faults near the southern coastline, this time running in an east–west direction, are responsible for forming the only high mountains in southern Western Australia, the Stirling Range. The range boasts five peaks more than 1,000 metres above sea level.

There are, however, other small peaks and ranges near the south coast, including Mt Frankland, Mt Roe, Mt Lindesay and the Porongurup Range. These are isolated granite outcrops, formed around the birth of the ancient continent of Gondwana and exposed by weathering of the surrounding plains. The Porongurup granites were formed about 1,184 million years ago, making this range one of the oldest in the world. When Antarctica finally separated from Australia about 50 million years ago, it resulted in the formation of a rugged and spectacular southern coastline of headlands, cliffs and granite peaks.

The climate of the South West is classified as Mediterranean, with cool, wet winters and warm to hot, dry summers. Temperatures in January or February can rise to 40°C, although this rarely occurs in the far south. In July, maximum temperatures are usually in the mid teens, and in some areas, like the Blackwood River valley, minimum temperatures can drop below freezing. The south coast can be windy, cold and bleak in winter and the Stirling Range occasionally gets snow, but in general the climate of the South West is relatively mild and pleasant all year round. In the north of the region, there is an almost total drought for about five months of the year over summer, but southern areas do experience periods of rain in the hotter months. The wettest part of the South West is the south coast near Walpole, which receives more than 1,400 millimetres of rain every year, while Bunbury has 880 millimetres and Margaret River 1,244 millimetres annually. Most of the rainfall is between May and October, originating from low-pressure systems and their associated cold fronts.

The plants of the South West are well adapted to this Mediterranean climate, with its dry summers and relatively frequent fires. The South West has been isolated from the rest of Australia for millions of

OPPOSITE White spider orchid (*Caladenia longicauda*), Stirling Range.
LEFT TOP Southern heath monitors are one of the reptile species that may be spotted in the South West.
LEFT BOTTOM Granny bonnets (*Isotropis cuneifolia*), Stirling Range.

21

Surfing is a way of life for many people in the South West.

years by deserts, resulting in a staggering diversity of plant life in the region. The South West Botanical Province is one of the richest non-tropical wild-flower areas in the world. Extending south and west of a line from Shark Bay to Israelite Bay, it has an estimated 7,000–9,000 species of flowering plants, with 80 per cent of them endemic to the region—that is, they are found nowhere else. Common plants are banksias, dryandras and hakeas of the Proteaceae family; eucalypts, melaleucas and bottlebrushes of the Myrtaceae family; heaths of the Epacridaceae family; and peas of the Papilionaceae family. Orchids (Orchidaceae family) are also found in profusion, along with triggerplants (Stylidiaceae family), acacias (Mimosaceae family) and grass trees (*Kingia* and *Xanthorrhoea* species).

The main vegetation groups of the South West are botanically rich heathlands found in coastal areas, and extensive eucalypt forests in the interior, dominated by tuart, jarrah, marri or karri trees. There are relatively small areas of banksia and peppermint woodlands on the Swan Coastal Plain and south coast, as well as salt lake communities in some areas. Granite outcrops provide a habitat for mosses, lichens and pincushions, along with larger plants like sheoaks, wattles and tea-trees. The Stirling Range harbours an area of *kwongan* (heathland), which is extraordinarily rich in endemic species.

There are many beautiful and unique forest habitats in the South West. Mixed jarrah and marri forests are found in the north and east of the region, merging into wandoo woodlands in eastern areas where the rainfall is less than 650 millimetres. Less common trees found in the jarrah forest are bullich, flooded gum and blackbutt. Karri occurs in a belt from near Nannup to Denmark, but there are also outlying populations at Margaret River, in the Porongurup Range and on Mt Manypeaks. Karri grows in magnificent tall forests, with the tallest trees more than 80 metres high, and often occurs in association with marri. In the far south around Walpole, the mighty karris share the forest with giant tingle trees, which have even larger buttressed trunks but do not grow as tall. Finally, the grey-barked tuarts of the Swan Coastal Plain occur in scattered pockets; there is only one remaining extensive tuart forest, near Ludlow. All of these forest communities grow naturally only in Western Australia.

The South West also has a wealth of animal life. There are more than 200 species of bird, the most spectacular including the red-tailed black cockatoo, brilliant blue splendid fairy wren, golden whistler, scarlet robin, tawny frogmouth, western rosella and wedge-tailed eagle. More than thirty mammal species are found in the region, such as the woylie, quenda, brushtail and western ringtail possums, chuditch, phascogale, dunnart, quokka and western grey kangaroo. The South West is a home for many reptile and amphibian species, and thousands of varieties of insects and other invertebrates. Common reptiles are bobtail skinks, dragon lizards and snakes, including the poisonous, but rarely seen, dugite and tiger snakes. Marron and the introduced rainbow and brown trout are found in many of the region's rivers.

With the exception of western grey kangaroos, most of the other mammal species are far more rare today than they were when Europeans first arrived on these shores. This is due in part to the clearing of areas of natural bush habitat, but also to predation from introduced foxes and feral cats. One of the largest wildlife recovery programs in the world has recently begun to reduce the numbers of these predators in the South West (and other areas of Western Australia). Called 'Western Shield', it involves the use of baits containing the poison 1080, which is found naturally in native pea plants of the genus *Gastrolobium*. Native animals have an inbuilt resistance to the toxin, acquired over thousands of years, while introduced animals like foxes, dogs, cats and livestock are highly susceptible to it. Synthetic 1080 in meat baits is now used extensively throughout the South West for the control of introduced predators. I have already seen the positive effects of this program for myself, in the increased numbers of marsupials like quenda, chuditch and possums at favourite camping sites like Honeymoon Pool near Collie. It is my hope that through programs such as 'Western Shield', young Western Australians in the future will become familiar with their unique animal species by contact with them in the wild, rather than only seeing them in zoos.

The South West is a region of great diversity and beauty. Most people here are relaxed and genuine, and warm country hospitality is found almost everywhere. They enjoy an active outdoor lifestyle and a generally temperate climate all year round. The sea and inland waterways are an important part of the lives of many people. There is a strong 'water culture' in the South West: swimming, sailing, diving, canoeing, surfing, boating and fishing are all popular. Locals and visitors also pursue land-based leisure activities like bushwalking, horse riding and cycling.

The following chapters cover four distinct parts of the region, each with its own character and special attractions. So join me now as I explore the South West—from dawn till dusk.

The Bunbury and Peel region

This area extends from the inlets and estuaries of Mandurah to just south of Bunbury, the commercial capital of the South West. The region boasts beautiful swimming beaches, forested hills, white-water rivers and productive farmland.

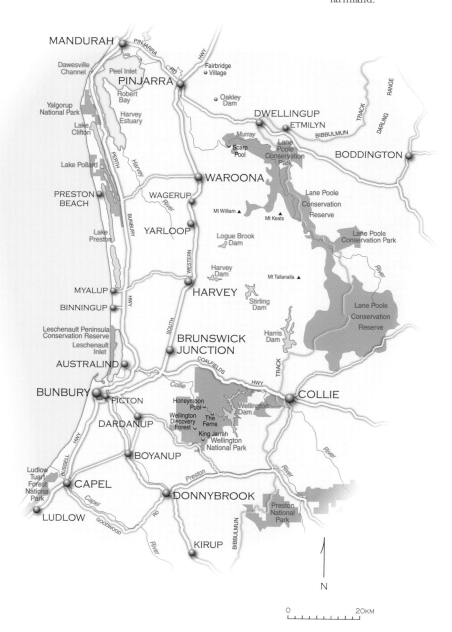

MANDURAH
PINJARRA RD
HWY
Dawesville Channel
Peel Inlet
Fairbridge Village
PINJARRA
Robert Bay
Oakley Dam
Yalgorup National Park
Harvey Estuary
DWELLINGUP
ETMILYN
BIBBULMUN
DARLING RANGE
TRACK
Lake Clifton
Murray
BODDINGTON
Scarp Pool
Lane Poole Conservation Park
Lake Pollard
PERTH
Harvey
WAROONA
PRESTON BEACH
WAGERUP
River
Lane Poole Conservation Reserve
Mt William ▲
BUNBURY
Lake Preston
YARLOOP
Logue Brook Dam
Mt Keats ▲
Lane Poole Conservation Park
River
WESTERN
Harvey Dam
Mt Tallanalla ▲
MYALUP
HWY
HARVEY
Stirling Dam
Lane Poole Conservation Reserve
BINNINGUP
Harris Dam
Leschenault Peninsula Conservation Reserve
SOUTH
BRUNSWICK JUNCTION
Leschenault Inlet
COALFIELDS
AUSTRALIND
Collie
HWY
TRACK
COLLIE
BUNBURY
PICTON
Honeymoon Pool
Wellington Dam
DARDANUP
Wellington Discovery Forest
The Ferns
King Jarrah
Wellington National Park
River
BUSSELL
BOYANUP
Preston
Ludlow Tuart Forest National Park
CAPEL
Capel
DONNYBROOK
Preston National Park
River
LUDLOW
GOODWOOD
RD
BIBBULMUN
River
KIRUP

N

0   20KM

Chapter 1

THE BUNBURY AND PEEL REGION

To most Perth residents, the South West begins at the holiday resort town of Mandurah. This is where the stress of the city, with its traffic congestion and peak hours, is left behind, and where the simpler, slower pace of country life begins. Mandurah is a beautiful town situated 75 kilometres south of Perth on the calm, protected waters of Peel Inlet and Harvey Estuary. To the south, the Swan Coastal Plain stretches down to the capital city of the South West, Bunbury, and is bordered in the east by the low rampart of the Darling Scarp. This is the Bunbury and Peel region, a place with a relaxed lifestyle and limitless opportunities for recreation. The many estuaries and inlets of the area provide excellent fishing, crabbing and prawning, as well as many water sports. The region is bounded in the west by the safe swimming beaches of the Indian Ocean, and the farming areas under the Darling Scarp are some of the most fertile in Western Australia. The scarp itself is a place of extensive jarrah and marri forests, numerous water catchment dams and rugged river valleys. Bushwalking is popular here, along with white-water rafting and canoeing in rivers like the Murray and Collie. The hills are a source of bauxite, coal and timber, which generate some of the main industries of the region. Agriculture and tourism are also important to the region's economy.

Even before European settlement, **Mandurah** was popular with visitors: the Aboriginal word 'mandjar', from which 'Mandurah' is derived, means 'meeting or trading place'. Aborigines came here for many of the reasons that thousands of tourists do today: the inlets provided abundant seafood, a wealth of wildlife and the chance to trade and socialize. Perhaps they also enjoyed relaxing here in this place of plenty. Today the waterways are often a hive of activity, with people swimming, yachting, boating, fishing and water skiing. The famous blue manna crabs are just one of the many seafood delicacies available for catching or sampling by visitors.

The first Europeans arrived in Mandurah in 1830 when Thomas Peel started an ambitious settlement scheme in the area. Peel, the cousin of a British Prime Minister, Sir Robert Peel, was originally promised land on the Swan and Canning rivers, but by the time his ships arrived in December 1829 the land had already been allocated. He instead took up 250,000 acres (101,250 hectares) from Rockingham to the Peel Inlet and east to the Darling Scarp. With his servants and settlers, he moved first to Woodman Point and then established a settlement at Mandurah. Peel had numerous problems, not the least of which were raids by Murray River (Binjareb) Aborigines, who mounted a guerrilla campaign against the settlement, spearing stock and damaging buildings with fire. One of his original settlers, a man named McKenzie, was speared to death in 1830. Peel's

A chilly dawn at Nanga Mill campsite, Lane Poole Conservation Reserve.

grand plans for his settlement ultimately failed, with most of his servants and settlers deserting him, but Mandurah itself survived and today is one of the fastest growing towns in the State.

The town centre is situated on the tranquil waters of the Mandurah Estuary, with pleasant parks and a laidback holiday atmosphere. The area is home to many aquatic bird species, for which the surrounding wetlands provide natural breeding grounds. I especially enjoy watching the giant pelicans, which strut around the main street, cafes and foreshore reserve as if they own the town. They look too ungainly to fly but are surprisingly graceful once they take to the air — very similar to a jumbo jet! The town has many new housing and canal developments, and major new buildings like the Performing Arts Centre and the Peel Discovery Centre, which displays the social and natural history of the area.

The vast inland waterways of the Peel Inlet and Harvey Estuary, covering an area of more than 90 square kilometres, experienced severe problems with algal blooms in the 1980s and early 1990s. The waterways are fed by the Murray, Serpentine and Harvey rivers, which have their headwaters in the agricultural inland areas. Fertilizers and other chemicals are washed into the inland waterways, promoting the excess growth of algae. The only natural outlet to the sea, the Mandurah Estuary, does not allow sufficient flushing of the waterways. To counteract this, the Dawesville Channel, a second outlet to the sea, was constructed to increase the tidal flow and help preserve the health of the inlet. Since being opened in 1994, the channel has been effective in preventing algal blooms but has had some side effects, such as increased salinity in the estuaries and damage to some of the fringing vegetation.

One of the main rivers feeding into the Peel Inlet is the Murray. This large, permanent river is one of the last in the northern jarrah forest spared from damming for water storage (primarily because it is too saline). The Murray is formed by the junction of the Hotham and Williams rivers, which both have their source near Narrogin in the Western Australian Wheatbelt. It flows through a major valley in the ancient hills of the Darling Range before reaching the coastal plain near Waroona. Much of this area is protected by the 54,000 hectare Lane Poole Conservation Reserve (a proposed national park), named after C. E. Lane Poole, the State's first Conservator of Forests. The Murray valley is a tranquil, beautiful place. There are numerous camping areas along the banks of the river where you can swim, walk in the bush or fish for marron, rainbow trout, redfin perch and cobbler. The river is a series of quiet pools in summer, but in winter its numerous large, foaming rapids make it popular for canoeing and white-water rafting. The Bibbulmun Track passes through the valley, and there are other bushwalks through the jarrah, marri and blackbutt forests.

Just north of Lane Poole Reserve lies the historic timber town of **Dwellingup**, founded in the late 1800s as a tiny mill settlement as the vast tracts of virgin jarrah in the northern forests began to be exploited. In World War II, the nearby settlement of Marrinup was the site of a prisoner of war camp, with thousands of German and Italian prisoners of war passing through between 1943 and 1946. On 24 January 1961, Dwellingup experienced the inferno of a bushfire that almost resulted in its complete destruction. In the middle of a long, hot summer, a lightning storm ignited five separate blazes in the tinder-dry jarrah forest. These fires eventually converged into one gigantic front more than 16 kilometres long. In spite of the efforts of local volunteer bushfire brigades and the Forest Department, the fire razed most of Dwellingup, leaving only the hotel and a few homes unscathed, and destroyed smaller towns in the area like Nanga Brook. Eventually, after five long days, the blaze was brought under control. One of the legacies of the Dwellingup fire is that planned burn-offs with low-intensity fires are carried out today in the South West forests, with the aim of reducing the risk of severe bushfires.

Dwellingup shows few signs of this disaster. The town has been rebuilt, with a small timber mill and the Department of Conservation and Land Management's Forest Heritage Centre. The heritage centre showcases the jarrah forest and its timber production—in particular, the expanding fine wood industry. Seen from the air, the centre looks like a tree bough with three buildings shaped like leaves.

Bauxite mining is another industry in this part of the South West. Mining began in the 1960s, with bauxite from the Darling Range near Dwellingup transported to a Pinjarra refinery for processing into alumina. Gold is also mined near the small, picturesque town of Boddington on the Hotham River, a tributary of the Murray.

Dwellingup is the destination of one of the most popular rail journeys in Western Australia. The Hotham Valley Tourist Railway runs from Pinjarra up and over the jarrah-forested Darling Scarp to Dwellingup. During winter and spring, when the fire danger is not high, tourists can enjoy the nostalgia of a steam-powered train. At other times of the year, diesel engines are used. A steam-powered tram with a dining car also operates between Dwellingup and Etmilyn from May to October.

The Murray River finally breaks through the Darling Range near Waroona and then meanders north over the coastal plain towards the town of **Pinjarra**, which nestles on its banks. This is one of the oldest towns in Western Australia. Settlers took up grants along the Murray River from 1835, after a conflict at Pinjarra decimated the local Binjareb Nyoongar tribe and reduced the risk of resistance to settlement. There were many other small incidents between settlers and Aborigines in the South West, but the Pinjarra 'battle' is perhaps the most infamous.

Four Binjareb tribesmen were flogged and gaoled for a month after a successful raid on Shenton's Flour Mill (the Old Mill) in South Perth. As the four tribesmen had been apprehended when they approached Peel's Mandurah settlement, the Aborigines believed Peel responsible for the arrests and tried to lure him into the bush by releasing several of his valuable mares. Peel did not go himself but sent Private Hugh Nesbit and Edward Barton to track the horses. They were ambushed by an Aboriginal party, resulting in Nesbit being killed.

Lake Clifton is one of only three sites in Western Australia where
ancient life forms known as thrombolites are found.

The shoreline at Lake Clifton, showing the transition from salt lake margin to rushes and sedges, *Melaleuca* paperbarks, and finally large tuart trees.

In 1834, Governor Stirling and Surveyor John Septimus Roe led a party to the Murray River to punish the offenders. The party of twenty-six included Thomas Peel, Captain Ellis and a detachment of soldiers from the 21st Regiment. An Aboriginal camp was found near the banks of the river, and Ellis and four troopers approached the Nyoongars on horseback to ascertain whether they were those responsible for the killing. The rest of the party took up a strategic position on the opposite high bank of the river. Ellis and his men thought they recognized one or more of the perpetrators and charged the camp of about seventy men, women and children. They shot a number of Aborigines, and Ellis received a spear blow to the skull, knocking him off his horse. The rest of the tribe fled across the river to where Governor Stirling and the other soldiers were waiting. As the first warriors ascended the steep bank on the far side, they were surprised by the troopers and forced back into the river. They then found themselves in a deadly crossfire, trapped in the river or below the steep banks by the two groups of soldiers, and most were cut down. Only eight women and a number of children were spared. Captain Ellis died later from his wound, but he was the only European casualty.

The massacre was justified later by Governor Stirling, who said that 'there was a danger that their success in this species of warfare might tempt other tribes to pursue the same course, and eventually combine together for the extermination of the whites'.* Along with this rather irrational fear, Stirling had a political motivation: he hoped to establish a line of garrisons linked by road between Perth and Albany, and the Binjareb Nyoongars stood in its way.

In October 2001, descendants of the original tribe, in the Murray Districts Aboriginal Association, officially opened a monument at Pinjarra in remembrance of this conflict.

The Pinjarra area is rich and fertile, and the new settlers prospered, as is evidenced by the fine historical buildings in the town. Many of these are located in the 'Edenvale' complex, where visitors today can experience a little of what the old town must have been like. This group of buildings includes St John's Anglican Church, built in 1861; the stately 'Edenvale' homestead, built in 1888 by Edward and Mary Ann McLarty; and the Old School House, built in 1862 next to the church. Other nearby historic buildings are 'Old Blythewood', 4 kilometres south of Pinjarra and built around 1860, and 'Fairbridge Village', a farm school for orphaned British children established in 1912 by Kingsley Fairbridge.

---

* Quoted in Murray Districts Aboriginal Association, *The Pinjarra Massacre*, pamphlet, Pinjarra, 1998.

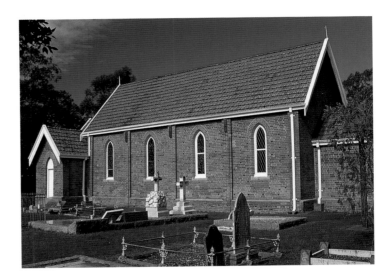

The historic St John's Anglican Church in Pinjarra, built in 1861.

Late afternoon light on paddocks near Pinjarra, with the rocky Darling Scarp rising behind.

South of Mandurah, the coastline curves along a limestone ridge, which then descends to the long, narrow and salty lakes of the Yalgorup National Park. This chain of salt lakes and swamps includes Lakes Preston and Clifton, which are remarkable for their wealth of bird life, including many migratory birds like the red necked stint from Siberia and the rainbow bird from the Solomon Islands and New Guinea. The lakes are more than seven times as salty as the sea, and Lake Clifton is one of only three sites in Western Australia where ancient 'living rocks' known as thrombolites are found. Thrombolites are composed of microbes, like bacteria and blue-green algae, which form mats of sticky film in the shallow water of the lake. These mats trap sediment particles and precipitate calcium carbonate, with the 'rock' growing about a millimetre each year. Fossil thrombolites and the related stromatolites are the oldest known form of organized cellular life on earth. Yalgorup National Park also has camping and picnic areas, along with some excellent bushwalks (see appendix) that wind over coastal dunes and through tuart groves to the lakes.

There are only three small beach towns between Mandurah and Bunbury: Preston Beach, Myalup and Binningup. These seem almost lost in time, retaining the atmosphere of the relaxed coastal retreats common in yesteryear. There is little of the rampant development seen further down the coast at places like Busselton and Dunsborough, although change may be inevitable. The beaches are all sheltered and offer safe swimming, beach fishing and some surfing. Myalup is a favoured place for hang-gliding enthusiasts, who jump from high sand dunes behind the beach.

Further down the coast is the Leschenault Peninsula Conservation Reserve, an important refuge for the rare western ringtail possum. The reserve protects a narrow strip of land between the Leschenault Estuary and the sea, with sand dunes, peppermint trees and tuart forests. Most of the peninsula has no vehicular access, although boating across from Australind to secluded spots in the reserve is popular.

Moving back inland, we pass the towns of Waroona, Yarloop, Harvey and Brunswick Junction, situated in the midst of rich farmland at the foot of the Darling Scarp. The hills behind the towns are a natural leisure area, with their forests, rivers and water catchment dams. Bushwalking, power boating, water skiing and trout fishing are all favourite pastimes, while marron can be caught in season. The **Waroona** shire has sheep and cattle farms, as well as irrigated market gardens in some areas. At **Yarloop**, an old timber town, there is a historical engineering workshop, dating from the horse and steam era, that has been restored and is now open to the public. **Brunswick Junction**, located south of Harvey on a rail junction, is an important dairying centre.

The **Harvey** region has some of the finest agricultural country in Western Australia and is famous for its dairy and beef cattle and citrus orchards. In the nearby hills of the Darling Range are the popular recreation areas of Logue Brook Dam and Harvey Dam. In 1999, work began on greatly increasing the size of Harvey Dam, and a concert amphitheatre and picnic facilities are planned. These facilities are designed to replace those at Stirling Dam, which was connected to Perth's water supply system in 2001 and so is now off-limits for recreation. In 1885, the creator of *Snugglepot and Cuddlepie*, May Gibbs, lived in Harvey, and 'Stirling's Cottage' is a replica of her original home. The cottage, located behind the Harvey Tourist Centre, has

tea-rooms, history displays, and arts and crafts with the gumnut theme. Another historical site in town is the Internment Camp Shrine built by Italian prisoners of war during World War II.

Just north of Bunbury, on the banks of the picturesque Leschenault Estuary near the mouth of the Collie River, lies the historic small town of **Australind**. This area was chosen in 1839 by the West Australian Land Company as a site for an intensive farming colony. A large party of settlers, led by Marshall Waller Clifton and his wife, Elinor, arrived on 18 March 1841 on the ship *Parkfield*. Unfortunately, the project all but collapsed after only two years due to a combination of the chronic labour shortage and the settlers' lack of understanding of Western Australian growing conditions. The company soon got into financial difficulties and was wound up. However, the town still retains some buildings constructed around this time. The Church of St Nicholas started out as a workman's cottage in 1842 and was converted to a church six years later. This intimate building, measuring just 3.8 metres by 6.7 metres, is thought to be the smallest church in Western Australia. Just opposite is 'Henton Cottage',

ABOVE Two antique W-class steam locomotives pulling the Hotham Valley Tourist Railway train up the steep Darling Scarp to Dwellingup. (This photograph was taken using a telephoto lens—I was not in danger of being crushed!)

OVER PAGE A rare area of old growth jarrah in the northern forests, protected recently in the Preston National Park near Donnybrook.

OPPOSITE Bunbury at dusk, with the Lord Forrest Hotel and the Bunbury Tower prominent.

ABOVE The Collie River is popular with canoeists all year round, because of the release of water to power the hydro-electric plant on the Wellington Dam.

LEFT The beautiful grey textured bark of a giant tuart tree (*Eucalyptus gomphocephala*) in the Ludlow Tuart Forest National Park.

built in 1841 as the Prince of Wales Hotel. 'Upton House', another of the town's historic buildings, was built by Marshall Waller Clifton in 1843. Today Australind is a relaxed holiday town famous for its excellent fishing, boating, sailing and windsurfing.

Bunbury, the capital and commercial centre of the South West, is a pleasant harbour town situated on a peninsula. The area was first explored in depth by the French in 1803. Nicolas Baudin, commander of the *Geographe*, discovered the Leschenault Inlet and named it after his botanist, Jean Baptiste Leschenault.

Soon after the founding of Perth, Governor Stirling set out in the man-of-war *Sulphur* to explore the area. He met up with Lieutenant Henry William St Pierre Bunbury at Port Leschenault in December 1836. Bunbury had just blazed an overland trail from Pinjarra, and the proposed town was named after him in honour of this feat. The first town lots were surveyed in 1841. The port gradually grew in importance to become the main outlet for the timber industry of the South West, and for the export of mineral sands from Capel, bauxite and alumina from the Darling Range and agricultural produce from the hinterland. Bunbury today, with a population of more than 28,000, is the second largest urban area in Western Australia.

One of Bunbury's most popular visitor attractions is the Dolphin Discovery Centre on Koombana Bay. Wild bottlenose dolphins visit the beach in front of the centre on an average of 250 days a year, and visitors can swim or snorkel with them under ranger supervision. The best time to see the dolphins is between 8.00 a.m. and noon. The centre also has an audio-visual show and an eco-museum. Bunbury, along with Monkey Mia near Shark Bay, is one of the few places in the world where visitors can interact with these beautiful marine mammals in their natural environment. Dolphins can also often be seen surfing the bow waves on cruises available along the calm waters of Koombana Bay.

The main street of Bunbury, Victoria Street, is well worth a visit. Many of its buildings, including the impressive Rose Hotel, built in 1865, have been restored to their former glory, and the area is enhanced by sculptures and harbour theme street-scaping. Victoria Street has many excellent sidewalk cafes and restaurants. At one end, the street is dominated by the Bunbury Tower, the city's first skyscraper, while the southern end is over-looked by the large St Patrick's Catholic Cathedral, completed in 1921. Only 50 metres away, across a road, is the Anglican Cathedral of St Boniface. The Old Post Office and Court House on Stephen Street is one of the city's oldest buildings, having been in use since 1855, and is now listed with the National Trust of Australia. Bunbury is very compact, and most attractions are within easy walking distance of the city centre. The beaches of the Indian Ocean are less than a kilometre away to the west, while Leschenault Inlet is only a few hundred metres to the east of Victoria Street.

The historic Rose Hotel in Bunbury, built in 1865.

ABOVE The basaltic rocks at Bunbury were formed from a volcanic lava flow that occurred about 150 million years ago.

OVER PAGE Dusk at Oakley Dam, above Pinjarra. This dam, built right on the edge of the Darling Scarp, supplies water to the Pinjarra alumina refinery on the coastal plain below.

A trip to the Boulters Heights or Marlston Hill lookout will give you an appreciation of Bunbury and its surrounds. From these small limestone ridges there are excellent views over the city and its extensive waterways to the Darling Scarp in the east. Marlston Hill is the site of the original Bunbury lighthouse, which served for thirty-three years before being replaced in 1903. The modern lighthouse was moved slightly to the south of Marlston Hill in 1971 and overlooks one of Bunbury's many ocean beaches. Near here are the basaltic rocks of Rocky Point, one of only two places in the ancient landscape of Western Australia where basalt can be seen above the ground. The black igneous rocks exposed on the beach were formed from a volcanic lava flow that occurred about 150 million years ago. To the south of these rocks, the long, golden beaches continue down towards Geographe Bay, with some popular swimming, fishing and surfing spots.

Another side to Bunbury is its wetlands, which provide a natural habitat for waterbirds and other

ABOVE A honeysuckle (*Lambertia multiflora*), found in heathland areas of the Darling Scarp.
LEFT Dusk in the Harvey area, famous for its beef cattle industry.

wildlife. Leschenault Inlet to the north and Big Swamp to the south of the city are important natural environments in the midst of this urban area. Leschenault Inlet is home to a remarkable relict mangrove colony, the most southerly in Western Australia. The nearest other occurrence is at the Abrolhos Islands, more than 500 kilometres to the north. A boardwalk constructed through the mangrove and samphire wetlands allows visitors to view some of the sixty waterbird species found here. The Big Swamp Reserve also has an elevated boardwalk, with viewing points and bird hides. Common birds seen here include black swans, herons, ibises, ducks and spoonbills.

The historic 'King Cottage', on Forrest Avenue, was built by brick maker Henry King in 1880. It is open to the public and has period furniture and displays of memorabilia. The avenue gets its name from 'Big John Forrest', Western Australia's first Premier and one of the fathers of federation, who was born at Preston Point near Bunbury in 1847.

ABOVE Kangaroo paws (*Anigozanthos manglesii*), Western Australia's floral emblem, are common throughout the South West.
BELOW Lush spring paddocks in the hills above Dardanup. The yellow flowers are cape weed, a problem weed species in the South West originally from South Africa.

Pelicans are very much a part of the Mandurah landscape.

The clear, blue waters of the Mandurah estuary are a popular place for
boating and fishing, with commercial cruises available to the Peel Inlet
and lower Murray River.

Five kilometres south-east of Bunbury, at Picton, is the second oldest church in Western Australia. St Mark's Church was built in 1842, by Reverend John Ramsden Wollaston, out of pit-sawn timber and wattle and daub. Wollaston was apparently told that he would not get his stipend of 100 pounds per annum from the British Government until he had completed a place of worship. With this sort of incentive, he managed to build the church—mainly with his own hands—within twelve months of arriving.

A recommended drive from Bunbury is over the Darling Scarp towards Collie. Some of the views from the main road as you crest the scarp are dramatic, with deeply incised valleys on both sides. A side road leads down to the scenic Collie River valley and lovely camping and picnic spots like Honeymoon Pool and the Ferns. I have spent many relaxed evenings in this area, with wild quenda and chuditch wandering freely through my camp. Further up the valley is the large Wellington Dam, the site of southern Western Australia's only hydro-electric plant. Canoeing is possible on the Collie River all year round because of the release of water to run this plant. There are some excellent bushwalks available in the Collie valley, along the river itself or to vantage points in the surrounding hills (see, for example, the Sika circuit, in the appendix). Much of this area has been protected in the recently proclaimed 17,500 hectare Wellington National Park.

Collie, some 54 kilometres east of Bunbury, is an important town. It is the only coalmining centre in Western Australia and has the largest open cut coalmine in the southern hemisphere. Coal was first discovered in 1883, and the Collie town site was founded in 1896. The last working underground mine shut in 1965 after being flooded, although there is a replica mine adjacent to the Steam Locomotive and Coalfields Museums in the town. Collie has some historic buildings including the Old Post Office, built in 1898, and the Court House, in use since 1913. The Bibbulmun Track passes close to the town, and just south of the town on the Collie River is Minninup Pool, a popular swimming and fishing hole.

South of the Collie River lies the rich farmland and forest area of Dardanup and the Ferguson valley. This is part of the emerging viticultural area of the Geographe wine region, with vineyards in the Ferguson valley and at Capel and Harvey. Dardanup itself is a historic town with fifteen heritage sites, including the hotel, convent and churches. In the upper Ferguson valley is one of at least three 'King Jarrah' trees in the South West, an enormous straight trunked jarrah some 36 metres high that dwarfs the

The Murray River leaves the hills near Waroona and winds across the
landscape to empty into the Peel Inlet.

The rugged Collie River valley at dusk, seen from the Coalfields Highway.

regrowth forest around it. The original old growth forest must have been spectacular. Virtually all of the northern jarrah forest is regrowth, with only minuscule areas left unscathed after 120 to 150 years of logging.

Wellington Mill was the first mill in the Ferguson valley, opening in 1881. The Wellington Discovery Forest, near the 'King Jarrah' tree, explains the diverse ecosystem of the jarrah forest and how it thrives in infertile soils in spite of fire and the annual summer drought. The jarrah and marri forest in this area is home to more than seventy bird species and mammals like the western grey kangaroo, chuditch, western ringtail possum and quenda. One of the problems the jarrah forest has faced since the 1960s is dieback, a plant disease caused by an introduced subtropical fungus, *Phytophthora cinnamomi*. This fungus seriously affects jarrah by attacking its root system and can lead to death of trees due to lack of water uptake by the roots. Dieback affects a wide range of other plants, and South West habitats like the southern heathlands are also under threat, as they harbour many susceptible species.

Another beautiful forest of the South West is found at Ludlow, just south of Capel. The stately tuart trees here are protected in the 2,280 hectare Ludlow Tuart Forest National Park, the largest remaining natural tuart forest in the world. Tuarts, which only grow on coastal limestone soils, are endemic to south-western Australia but have been used as a plantation tree in parts of the Middle East. The national park has an open, park-like atmosphere, with majestic, grey-barked tuarts, some of which grow to more than 40 metres in height, dotting the landscape. The forest, with its peppermint tree understorey, boasts the highest density of brushtail and western ringtail possums in Western Australia.

Capel has dairy and beef cattle farms, and the surrounding soils are rich in ilmenite, rutile and zircon, making the area one of the primary sources of mineral sands in Western Australia. The mining company has rehabilitated some of the mine pits to form the Capel Wetlands Centre, a series of fourteen ponds with bird hides and viewing points, attracting fifty waterbird species and sixty species of bush birds. Capel also has safe swimming beaches on Geographe Bay, as well as a number of wineries.

To the south-east of Bunbury is the picturesque town of **Donnybrook**, founded in 1842 when a party of five Irishmen arrived in the district and named the green valley in reminiscence of home. Donnybrook is on the Preston River, which cuts a wide and gently rolling valley through the ancient hills of the Darling Range. Today this fertile area has

OVER PAGE Robert Bay in the early morning, Peel Inlet.

fruit, vegetable, cattle and sheep farms. Donnybrook is known as the apple centre of the South West and there are several fruit and grape wineries in the area. A famously potent drop known as 'Kirup Syrup' is produced nearby at the small town of Kirup. Historic buildings built from local granite stone include the Donnybrook Town Hall, and the Anchor and Hope Inn, which was established around 1862 as a staging inn for horse and cart travellers on their way to the Blackwood River valley and the tall forests—but that is another chapter! At this point we leave the Bunbury and Peel region, with its many attractions and leisure pursuits.

OPPOSITE Large marri trees reflected in the tranquil waters of the Collie River.

ABOVE In winter and spring, the Murray River boasts some of the best rafting and canoeing in Western Australia.

The South West capes

The capes region is bounded in the west by the rugged cliffs and surf beaches of the Leeuwin-Naturaliste Ridge, and extends inland to farmland, forest and some of the best wine country in Australia.

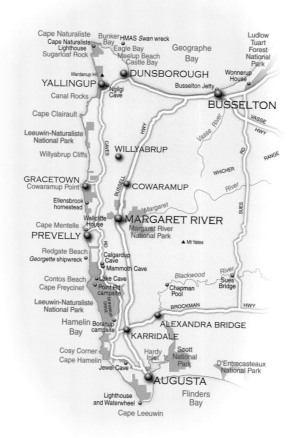

Cape Naturaliste
Bunker Bay
HMAS *Swan* wreck
Cape Naturaliste Lighthouse
Eagle Bay
Meelup Beach
Geographe Bay
Ludlow Tuart Forest National Park
Sugarloaf Rock
Castle Bay
Wardanup Hill
DUNSBOROUGH
Wonnerup House
YALLINGUP
Busselton Jetty
Ngilgi Cave
Canal Rocks
BUSSELTON
VASSE HWY
Cape Clairault
Vasse River
Leeuwin-Naturaliste National Park
CAVES RD
WILLYABRUP
WHICHER RANGE
Willyabrup Cliffs
WHICHER
River
GRACETOWN
BUSSELL RD
COWARAMUP
Cowaramup Point
SUES RD
Ellensbrook homestead
Margaret
Wallcliffe House
MARGARET RIVER
Cape Mentelle
Margaret River National Park
PREVELLY
▲ Mt Yates
Redgate Beach
CALDES RD
Calgardup Cave
Georgette shipwreck
Mammoth Cave
Blackwood
River
Contos Beach
Lake Cave
Chapman Pool
Sues Bridge
Cape Freycinet
Point Rd campsite
BORANUP DRIVE
Leeuwin-Naturaliste National Park
BROCKMAN HWY
Hamelin Bay
Boranup campsite
ALEXANDRA BRIDGE
KARRIDALE
Cosy Corner
Hardy Inlet
Scott National Park
Cape Hamelin
D'Entrecasteaux National Park
Jewel Cave
AUGUSTA
Lighthouse and Waterwheel
Flinders Bay
Cape Leeuwin

N

0   20KM

Chapter 2

THE SOUTH WEST CAPES

The magnificent peninsula between the scenic capes of Naturaliste and Leeuwin is one of the most popular tourist destinations in Western Australia. Every year, thousands of work-weary Perth citizens head south on pilgrimages to places like Busselton and Margaret River, to lie on the beach, taste the wines and enjoy the good life away from the bustling city. They are joined by overseas and interstate tourists, lured by the area's many attractions and its proximity to Perth. Along with the scenic coastline and stunning beaches, the region also boasts famous wineries, karri forests, rolling countryside and spectacular limestone caves. There are also restaurants, arts and craft centres and a wide variety of accommodation options. The capes region has something for everyone.

The area has been home for thousands of years to Nyoongar Aboriginal people, and their poetic language is evident in many of the region's names, such as Yallingup, Gnarabup, Boranup and Boodjidup. The first European contact with the region was in 1622, when a Dutch ship, the *Leeuwin*, was blown far south of its destination of Batavia. It is uncertain whether the crew went ashore, but there is some evidence of exploration, with a seventeenth-century Dutch clog being found at Flinders Bay in 1930. In 1801, the French ships *Geographe* and *Naturaliste*, under the command of Nicolas Baudin, visited the capes region. Many of the coastal names of the area, such as Freycinet, Mentelle and Clairault, are derived from this expedition. The Englishman Matthew Flinders passed Cape Leeuwin in December 1801, and the British were the first to settle in the region, at Augusta in 1830.

Busselton, 229 kilometres south of Perth, is the gateway to the South West capes. It has become a bustling town, with its own regional airport and a population of more than 10,000 people. In certain holiday periods it can be very busy, but for most of the year it retains its original charm as a relaxed seaside resort. Busselton was founded in 1832 when John Bussell and his family from the Augusta settlement relocated to the more hospitable country of the Vasse. Other Augusta pioneers like the Molloy, Chapman and Layman families soon followed.

The Layman family took up land around Busselton in 1834 and gradually wrested a farm from the bush, clearing the massive tuart trees by hand. In 1859 they built the stately 'Wonnerup House', now owned by the National Trust of Australia. Other buildings on the farm have been restored and opened to the public, including a one-teacher school and an earlier house, dating from 1837, that was later converted to a dairy and

Round-leaved pigface (*Disphyma crassifolium*) is common in coastal heathland areas in the South West.

The original house at Wonnerup, built by George Layman in 1837 and later converted to a dairy and kitchen.

kitchen. Another historic building in Busselton is the two-storey colonial style 'Prospect Villa', built in 1855 by James Chapman. St Mary's Church is one of the oldest in Western Australia, built between 1843 and 1845 from local limestone and pit-sawn timber.

Busselton is situated at the mouth of the Vasse River on the calm, protected waters of Geographe Bay. There are many excellent beaches here that have been favourite swimming and fishing spots for generations of Western Australians. To the east of Busselton are the Vasse-Wonnerup wetlands, a haven for many species of waterbird. One of the major landmarks of the area is the famous Busselton Jetty—at almost 2 kilometres, the longest timber jetty in Australia. Unfortunately, a fire in 2000 burnt about 70 metres of the end of the jetty, but there are plans to rebuild this area and also to construct an underwater observatory for visitors. The piles under

the jetty house unusual soft coral and sponge communities and attract many species of fish. It is an excellent place for fishing and scuba diving, or you can just stroll along the jetty or take the little train to the end. The jetty, which was first constructed to 175 metres in 1865 and reached its present length in 1960, was originally used for the export of timber from the South West forests.

Further around the curve of Geographe Bay is the resort town of **Dunsborough**. In common with Busselton, the town has grown rapidly in the last decade and has new housing subdivisions and golf courses to show for it. Hopefully, its laidback ambience will remain unchanged in spite of this. Dunsborough has its own sheltered beach on Geographe Bay and is also close to the superb swimming beaches of the eastern side of Cape Naturaliste. These bays, like Meelup Beach, Eagle Bay

ABOVE Cape Leeuwin was first sighted by the Dutch ship of the same name in 1622.

OVER PAGE Busselton Jetty at dawn.

and Bunker Bay, are a perfect spot for picnicking and for swimming in very safe waters. The high headland of the Leeuwin-Naturaliste Ridge protects these beaches from heavy ocean swells and from the prevailing south-westerly winds, resulting in lushly vegetated, Robinson Crusoe style coves.

One of my favourite places here is Castle Bay, a sweep of clean, white sand leading to the imposing granite headland of Castle Rock. It is hard to believe that such an idyllic spot was once the site of a whaling station, which operated in these waters from about 1845 to 1870. The whalers used the height of Castle Rock as a lookout point. Thankfully, these waters are still famous for their humpback whales, now hunted only by camera-wielding tourists who take whale-watching cruises during the spring season. From September, humpbacks pass through this area on their annual migration down the

Western Australian coast to their summer feeding grounds near Antarctica. Blue whales are also spotted occasionally in the waters off Cape Naturaliste. Another water-based attraction near Dunsborough is the wreck of the HMAS *Swan*, a decommissioned navy boat that was sunk some 1.3 nautical miles off Point Picquet on 14 December 1997. It is now a successful artificial reef and a dive site of world renown.

The Swan Coastal Plain ends near Dunsborough at the foot of the Leeuwin-Naturaliste Ridge. This limestone and granite coastal ridge extends almost 100 kilometres between the two prominent head-lands of Cape Naturaliste and Cape Leeuwin, rising in places to more than 200 metres above sea level. The base rock of the ridge is ancient granite more than 600 million years old. These hard, crystalline igneous rocks are highly resistant to erosion but often contain weak points, like joints, which allow

the formation of spectacular rock features such as Yallingup's Canal Rocks. Above the granite are beds of limestone, formed from consolidated sand dunes probably within the last 2 million years. Limestone is porous, and much of the drainage of the ridge is underground, with only larger streams like Margaret River and Willyabrup Brook forcing their way to the sea with surface flow. Over many thousands of years, most of the water has soaked into the ridge to form the famous caves, underground streams and drip-stone formations of the capes region.

There are around 350 caves in the Leeuwin-Naturaliste Ridge, many with beautiful stalactites, stalagmites, shawls and columns. Along with the semi-guided Ngilgi Cave at Yallingup, there are the guided Mammoth and Lake caves in the Boranup forest and the Jewel Cave near Augusta. Many other caves are accessible through adventure exploration companies. Some of these involve abseiling into the depths and then exploring with the light of head torches. This is great fun and highly recommended! Giants and Calgardup caves near Boranup are adventure caves you can explore by yourself, with the aid of a torch and a helmet.

The northern headland of Cape Naturaliste, 13 kilo-metres north-west of Dunsborough, is distinguished

ABOVE LEFT Spoonbills are one of many waterbird species that can be seen in the Vasse-Wonnerup wetlands near Busselton.
LEFT Vineyards at Wise Winery, near Dunsborough.

ABOVE An osprey uses the height of
Castle Rock as a lookout point for prey,
much like whalers would have done to
spot their quarry in the nineteenth
century.

RIGHT A brushtail possum at the Point
Road campsite.

OVER PAGE The beautiful turquoise
waters of Castle Rock beach near Cape
Naturaliste.

Limestone formations at Ngilgi Cave, Yallingup.

by its own lighthouse, built in 1903 from local limestone. There are some excellent bushwalking tracks leading to secluded beaches and scenic lookouts (see appendix).

Cape Naturaliste is the northernmost point of the Leeuwin-Naturaliste National Park, which stretches 100 kilometres almost without interruption to Cape Leeuwin. There are some superb scenic areas along this coast, where the power of the sea and its massive swells has worked its creative magic on the limestone and granite rocks. Sheer sea cliffs and rugged headlands are interspersed by unspoilt beaches of white sand. The national park, covering an area of almost 16,000 hectares, has wide variety. The heath-covered coastal areas give way to jarrah and karri forests in the lee of the hills, and to the underground limestone caves. The whole area is ablaze with wildflowers from late August to November. Not surprisingly, this national park is the most visited in Western Australia, with more than 1 million visitors every year.

A recent addition to the Leeuwin-Naturaliste National Park is the Cape to Cape Walk Track, beginning and ending at the two lighthouses of Capes Leeuwin and Naturaliste (see appendix). This 120 kilometre long walk track traverses high coastal cliffs, meanders along pristine beaches and occasionally heads inland to pass through verdant karri forests or to climb to high points on the Leeuwin-Naturaliste Ridge. It takes about a week to walk the whole distance, although many sections can be walked as day or half-day walks. Campsites are provided along the route,

ABOVE The beautiful Boranup karri forest, south of Margaret
River on Caves Road.
OVER PAGE Sugarloaf Rock, near Cape Naturaliste, is home to
the southernmost breeding colony of the endangered red-tailed
tropic bird.

The unusual pineapple bush (*Dasypogon hookeri*) is endemic to the Leeuwin-Naturaliste Ridge and the Whicher Range south of Bunbury.

ABOVE Canal Rocks, one of the impressive granite rock formations in the Yallingup area, formed by erosion of joints in the rocks.

OVER PAGE Typical coastline near Yallingup, with granite headlands and stunning white beaches.

many in remote areas away from roads and towns. I would recommend that everyone take at least a short stroll along the track, as it brings home how lucky we are to have such a magnificent wild coastline, still relatively free of development. In many other parts of the world, unspoilt coastlines are just a distant memory.

One of the spectacular formations along this coast is Sugarloaf Rock, a massive granite outcrop a couple of kilometres south of Cape Naturaliste. The rock is an important refuge for the red-tailed tropic bird, which is protected from attack by foxes and feral cats by the natural sea barrier. Sugarloaf Rock is the southernmost breeding site of this endangered seabird, usually found in tropical and subtropical seas around northern Australia and the Pacific.

Further south along the coast is the surfing and holiday town of **Yallingup**, situated on a beautiful beach 263 kilometres south of Perth. Many people believe that the Yallingup surf break is one of the best in Australia, and the beach also offers safe swimming in a sheltered rock pool. There are several other excellent surfing sites nearby. Yallingup is an Aboriginal word meaning 'place of love', and, appropriately, one of the main attractions of the area is the historic Caves House, which has been a favourite honeymoon venue for almost 100 years. The hotel was built by the State Government in 1903, and still offers accommodation, restaurants and bars. Early visitors used to travel by horse and buggy from Busselton along a dirt road, with the journey taking around three hours. The original

building was burnt in 1938, but the hotel was subsequently rebuilt. There is an interesting story about the path that runs down from the hotel along a collapsed limestone gorge to the sea. Called the 'Ghost Trail', it is said to be haunted by a beautiful Perth girl, one of the first guests to stay at the hotel, who had an unhappy love affair and fled down the track towards the sea, never to be seen again.

There are also Aboriginal legends about this area. The limestone Ngilgi Cave, only a couple of hundred metres from Caves House, was traditionally the home of an evil spirit, Wolgine. Aborigines were terrified of him, believing that he was responsible for the scarcity of food and water in the region. They were sure that if anyone entered the cave, they would die at the hand of Wolgine. A good spirit, Ngilgi, was enlisted to help, and he drove Wolgine into the main cavern of the cave with a great storm, eventually forcing him through the roof, and the evil spirit was banished forever. Ngilgi Cave is open to the public. Visitors may explore the cave at their own pace, but guides are available to answer any queries.

The coastline around Yallingup is scenic, with impressive granite formations like Canal and Torpedo rocks and many fine beaches. There are several wineries in the area, and some excellent bushwalks, including the Cape to Cape Walk Track.

Moving south again through lush, rolling countryside, we enter the important wine-growing area of the Willyabrup valley. The first vineyards were planted in the capes region in 1967, near the town of Cowaramup. Since then, wines from Willyabrup, Margaret River and Yallingup have achieved national and international recognition for their quality. The area is now one of the leading wine-producing regions in Australia, with more than fifty vineyards and thirty wineries, including famous names like Sandalford, Evans & Tate, Cape Mentelle and Vasse Felix. Many offer tastings and sales on site, often along with restaurants and art galleries. Leeuwin Estate, 9 kilometres south of Margaret River, even has its own internationally renowned concert. The first Leeuwin Concert was in 1985, and since then this event has grown to become a highlight of the South West social calendar. The setting is magnificent, with a backdrop of towering karri trees and, in good weather, thousands of stars in the clear night sky. Add to this the excellent music, food and wine and it is easy to see why the concert is so popular. Some of the biggest names in the entertainment industry have performed here over the years, such as Michael Crawford, Tom Jones, Dame Kiri Te Kanawa and John Farnham.

LEFT The 2001 Leeuwin Concert featured David Helfgott (performing here) and Roberta Flack.
OPPOSITE TOP Amazing limestone formations at Ngilgi Cave near Yallingup.
OPPOSITE BOTTOM Beautiful shawl formation, Ngilgi Cave.

Castle Rock, overlooking the idyllic beach of the same name.

The coastline of the capes region is famous for its excellent surf.

Margaret River, located 277 kilometres south of Perth in a rich dairy and beef cattle, winery and timber region, is one of the major tourism centres in Western Australia. The town is surrounded by gently rolling hills and forests, and is only a short distance inland from the rugged coastline. Margaret River has grown quickly over the last decade but retains its relaxed country ambience. It is still a surfers' town, with many surf shops along the main street. Craft shops also abound, featuring the work of local painters, potters, weavers, woodturners and carvers. Margaret River is a haven for people seeking an alternative, more laidback lifestyle to that usually found in big cities.

There are many excellent surf breaks along the coast near Margaret River, at places like Cowaramup Bay, the Margaret River mouth and Redgate. The surf here is renowned for its size, with waves as high as 3–4 metres in the right conditions. The area is a magnet to keen surfers from around the world, and hosts several major international surfing contests. The coast here also offers excellent conditions for windsurfing. If the waves are blown out by strong winds, windsurfers take their turn at tackling the sea, doing spectacular wave jumps and flying along at great speed. Other adventure activities such as abseiling and rock climbing are popular at places like the scenic Willyabrup Cliffs.

The region was pioneered by Alfred and Ellen Bussell and their family. Alfred Bussell was one of the original Augusta settlers, arriving in Western Australia in 1830. He established the 'Ellensbrook' homestead in 1857, on the coast just north of Margaret River, for his 16-year-old bride, Ellen. This historic building, built from crushed shell and limestone, is now managed by the National Trust of Australia and is open to the public. The Bussells lived there until 1865, when they moved to 'Wallcliffe House' at the mouth of the Margaret River.

Near 'Ellensbrook' homestead are the beautiful Meekadarribee Falls. Meekadarribee, which means 'the moon's bathing place', is the setting of an Aboriginal legend. A young girl named Mitanne enjoyed exploring caves and strange places, sometimes in the company of a boy called Nobel. Mitanne had been promised in marriage to a tribal elder. One day, she discovered the falls and excitedly told her clan that she had found the moon's bathing place. This angered her grandmother, because gazing on the moon in the water was said to bring death and sorrow. Mitanne and Nobel eloped together to Meekadarribee, where they hunted at night to avoid detection. One night, though, Nobel was speared by warriors sent by the elder, and he died in Mitanne's arms. She was forced back to the camp and a life of misery with the elder.

OPPOSITE The magical Meekadarribee Falls lie hidden away in a peppermint tree grotto near 'Ellensbrook' homestead.
RIGHT 'Ellensbrook' was the original homestead in the Margaret River area, built in 1857 by Alfred Bussell.

After she died, her spirit was reunited with Nobel's and they went back to the cave behind Meekadarribee Falls, where it is said they still reside.

Settlers were slow to arrive in the region until the timber industry boom of the 1890s. Margaret River town site was established in 1910, and expanded quickly in the 1920s with the introduction of the Group Settlement Scheme. 'Basildene Manor' is one of the stately homes of the area, built in 1912 by Percy Willmott, a lighthouse keeper at Cape Leeuwin. He used local granite and jarrah to create an elegant building, which is now classified by the National Trust of Australia.

Margaret River itself winds its way down to the sea near the small coastal resort town of **Prevelly**. There are some excellent swimming beaches here, like the Margaret River mouth and Gnarabup Beach, and one of the most famous surfing spots in Australia in the Margaret River main break. Prevelly holds many happy memories for me of lazy summer days spent swimming and walking along this beautiful coast. Near the mouth of the river is the heritage-listed 'Wallcliffe House', built in 1864. This has been restored and furnished with period pieces, although it is not open to the public. In this area, the Margaret River snakes through a deep, scenic valley in the Leeuwin-Naturaliste Ridge with limestone cliffs and small river beaches—an idyllic place for paddling a canoe laden with a picnic hamper and perhaps a bottle of wine!

Redgate Beach, south of Prevelly, was the scene of one of the most dramatic sea rescues in Western Australia's history. On 1 December 1876, the steam and sailing ship *Georgette* started to take on water on the way to Albany. Its pumps failed and the hold became flooded. One lifeboat launched beached safely at Quindalup, while a second boat capsized, drowning two women and six children. The survivors in the *Georgette* kept baling while the ship headed for the coast under sail. It grounded near Redgate and began to be battered on the rocks by the pounding surf. However, 16-year-old Grace Bussell (daughter of Alfred and Ellen) and a young Aboriginal stockman, Sam Isaacs, rode into the stormy sea and helped to get all fifty-three people on board safely to shore.

There are two main highways that travel south from the Margaret River area. The first is the Bussell

The Margaret River flows through an attractive valley near Prevelly,
where canoeing is popular.

Highway, which heads straight down to Augusta through gently rolling farmland and occasional patches of bush. However, I recommend travelling via Caves Road, which is only 10 kilometres longer and far more scenic. The road winds through forests, over hills and past coastal bays to Augusta, providing access to many caves along the Leeuwin-Naturaliste Ridge such as the Lake, Jewel, Giants and Mammoth caves. Short side trips take you to secluded beaches and high lookout points.

One of the most awe-inspiring areas along Caves Road is the Boranup karri forest, 20 kilometres south-west of Margaret River. This area was felled in the late 1800s to provide timber for the mills at Karridale. Today it is again a beautiful karri forest, with even-aged stands of trees in massed ranks. The forest is more open in places than those near Pemberton, with low understorey vegetation. One particularly breathtaking spot is where the road swings around a corner and the ground drops away to a valley filled with large karris. There are a number of small campsites in or near the forest at Boranup, Contos Field and Point Road. Boranup Drive is a scenic gravel road branching off from Caves Road, leading through the forest to a lookout and the Boranup camping area.

South of Boranup, Caves Road swings westward towards the coast, and there are side roads leading down to beautiful coastal spots like Hamelin Bay and Cosy Corner. Both bays offer good fishing and safe swimming beaches, where diving and snorkelling are possible. Just east of Cosy Corner are the guided Jewel Cave, boasting the longest straw stalactite of any tourist cave in the world, and the adventure guided Moondyne Cave. Nearby, Old Kudardup Cave (not accessible to the public) contains Aboriginal hand stencils, the only known example of painted rock art in the South West limestone caves.

Augusta is situated on the Hardy Inlet at the mouth of the Blackwood River, some 320 kilometres south of Perth. In March 1830, prospective free settlers arrived in Perth aboard the vessel *Warrior*, but unfortunately no more land was available for them. The situation was somewhat embarrassing for Governor Stirling, who subsequently led a group, including the Molloy, Bussell and Turner families, down to establish a new settlement in the Flinders Bay area, landing on 2 May 1830. Augusta was the third settlement in the fledgling Swan River Colony. The new arrivals had a hard time clearing the big jarrah and karri trees and found it impossible to grow enough food to support themselves. Supply ships were irregular, and communication with Perth difficult. Inevitably, the settlement failed, and most people moved to the Vasse area within a few years. A second wave of pioneers in the 1860s managed to re-establish the town. Maurice Coleman Davies established a timber empire in the 1870s, with karri cut at Boranup, milled at Karridale and shipped to London for use as street pavers. Jetties were built at Hamelin and Flinders bays for this export industry. Davies also built the Cape Leeuwin lighthouse, cottages and waterwheel, in association with a Mr Wishart, with the lighthouse foundation stone laid in 1895 by Sir John Forrest. The old waterwheel here is interesting, as its timber structure has gradually turned to limestone with the passage of time. It originally supplied natural spring water to the lighthouse keeper's cottage.

The lighthouse is situated 8 kilometres south of Augusta on the windswept granite headland of Cape Leeuwin. This stormy and often cold spot is where the Indian and Southern oceans meet. The cape was named by Matthew Flinders in 1801, after the Dutch ship *Leeuwin*. My first visit to Cape Leeuwin was memorable. A group of about thirty dolphins were working together in the shallows to herd a school of fish against the rocks of the headland. As they fed, they surfed the

Lush farmland and an abandoned settler's cottage near Augusta, with the Leeuwin-Naturaliste Ridge in the background.

waves that were breaking on the cape, and seemed to be having a great time! I spent a couple of enthralling hours watching and photographing their antics.

Flinders Bay offers excellent opportunities for whale watching, and commercial cruises are available. Humpback whales arrive from the south in late autumn on their journey up the Western Australian coast, while southern right whales arrive at the same time and breed along the southern coastline. Fur seals can also be seen on an island in Flinders Bay. Augusta was the site of one of the largest whale strandings recorded in Australia. One hundred and fourteen false killer whales became stranded on Deeres Beach in 1986, and Department of Conservation and Land Management officials and volunteers worked non-stop for sixty hours to return them to the ocean. In all, ninety-six whales were saved by this great community effort.

The Blackwood River is the longest permanent river in the South West, with its source near Kojonup and Arthur River, and its mouth at the Hardy Inlet near Augusta. Hardy Inlet has excellent fishing and water sports, and cruises are available to Molloy Island and the lower Blackwood River. Just upriver lie the tranquil camping spots of Alexandra Bridge, Chapman Pool and Sues Bridge, accessible by road or by boat. Excellent conditions for flat-water canoeing are found on the river all year round.

The lower Blackwood winds through extensive jarrah and marri forests, and the wild country known as the Donnybrook sunlands stretches north from the river to the low hills of the Whicher Range near Busselton. The sunlands (part of an ancient rift valley) are relatively low-lying and flat and extend eastwards to Nannup, where the southern end of the Darling Scarp formation again rises in rolling hills. Most of this area is State Forest, although national parks were recently proclaimed along the river itself. The sunlands are said to be the home of the legendary Nannup tiger, or thylacine, and many locals are convinced of its existence. It is said to stalk through the forests and into the surrounding farmlands, occasionally taking farm animals. Some claim to have seen the tiger, but no firm evidence exists. It remains one of the enduring mysteries of this part of the South West.

The tall forests

This region extends from the tiny settlement of Mullalyup at the northern boundary of the Blackwood River valley to the wild and beautiful southern coastline near Windy Harbour. Much of the area is dominated by tall forests of karri, jarrah and marri.

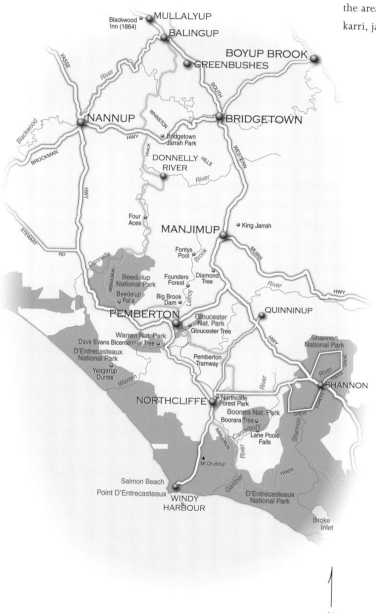

MULLALYUP
Blackwood Inn (1864)
BALINGUP
BOYUP BROOK
GREENBUSHES
VASSE
River
SOUTH
NANNUP
WHINSTON
BRIDGETOWN
Blackwood
BROCKMAN
HWY
TRACK
Bridgetown Jarrah Park
DONNELLY RIVER
HILLS
WESTERN
River
HWY
STEWART RD
Four Aces
MANJIMUP
King Jarrah
MUIRS
Donnelly
BIBULMUN
Fontys Pool
Brook
River
HWY
Beedelup National Park
Founders Forest
Diamond Tree
Beedelup Falls
Big Brook Dam
Lefroy
PEMBERTON
Gloucester Nat. Park
QUINNINUP
Shannon National Park
Warren Nat. Park
Gloucester Tree
Dave Evans Bicentennial Tree
HWY
River
D'Entrecasteaux National Park
Pemberton Tramway
THREES
FOREST
DRIVE
Yeagarup Dunes
Warren
River
SHANNON
NORTHCLIFFE
Northcliffe Forest Park
GREAT
Shannon
Boorara Nat. Park
BIBULMUN
Canterbury
River
Boorara Tree
Lane Poole Falls
TRACK
Mt Chudalup
River
Gardner
D'Entrecasteaux National Park
Salmon Beach
Point D'Entrecasteaux
WINDY HARBOUR
Broke Inlet

N

0   20KM

Chapter 3

THE TALL FORESTS

The tall forests region could be described as the kingdom of the karri. The area from Nannup to Northcliffe and the Shannon Basin is where the tall forests of the South West are at their most magnificent. The beautiful karri tree reaches its greatest height here, and occurs in an almost unbroken belt that extends to Denmark on the south coast. Other forest trees of the South West, like jarrah and marri, also grow taller here than they do in lower rainfall areas to the north and east. Most of the towns in the region, like Pemberton and Manjimup, historically owe their existence to the logging and processing of this rich timber resource. Agriculture is important, too, and the area has recently seen a phenomenal growth in tourism and related industries like viticulture. The tall forests region is bordered in the north by the beautiful Blackwood River valley, one of the most picturesque areas of Western Australia with its rolling hills, forests and rich farmland, and extends south to a rugged wilderness coast protected by the D'Entrecasteaux National Park.

Karri (*Eucalyptus diversicolor*) is the third tallest tree in the world, behind the redwood sequoia of California and the mountain ash of Tasmania and Victoria. These magnificent trees generally grow only in deep loam soils where the annual rainfall is higher than 1,100 millimetres. The tallest karri tree standing today is an 89 metre giant in the Warren National Park near Pemberton, and these trees can live as long as 350 or 400 years. For most of the year, karris have smooth ivory bark, but they shed it in autumn to reveal new bark with a beautiful salmon pink colour. To stand in a pristine forest of these towering trees is an awe-inspiring experience. I find it almost spiritual—you feel as though you are entering one of the ancient cathedrals in Europe and should speak in hushed tones and tread softly and gently. To fully appreciate this beauty, it is best to walk through the forest or explore it by other non-motorized means such as canoeing or biking.

Other trees in this region include the marri or redgum (*Corymbia calophylla*), which can grow as high as 60 metres in rich soils. Marris are often gnarled trees, with fire-blackened trunks and wounds in their bark oozing with thick, red gum. They are important nesting sites for native animals like possums and phascogales, as old trees usually have hollow trunks and branches. Jarrah (*Eucalyptus marginata*), with its characteristic striated bark, is another large tree in the region, growing up to 40 metres and living 300 to 600 years. The forest understorey is a blaze of colour in spring, from September to November. More than 1,500 species of wildflower are found in the southern forests, and about ninety-nine of these are endemic. Common species include the vivid red flowers of the coral vine (*Kennedia coccinea*), the delicate white flowering clematis

Marri trees below Mt Chudalup, D'Entrecasteaux National Park.

(*Clematis pubescens*), and hoveas and leschenaultias, with their purple and blue flowers. Many orchids are also found here, and other important understorey species are karri boronia (*Boronia gracilipes*), water-bushes (*Bossiaea* species), peppermint (*Agonis flexuosa*) and karri hazel (*Trymalium spathulatum*). A rainforest relic from Gondwanan times, the emu plum (*Podocarpus drouyniana*), is common in the karri and southern jarrah forests.

These unique forests are a priceless asset to Western Australia as tourists come to our shores in search of unaltered and unpolluted natural landscapes, which are becoming increasingly rare the world over. Ecotourism is a large growth industry in the South West. Forest industries like logging are still important in the region and, if managed in a sustainable way in plantation and regrowth forest areas, can continue indefinitely into the future. Recently, national parks

were gazetted to preserve the remaining 10 per cent of our original old growth forests for the benefit of future generations. This is a great step forward for the South West. It is true that you can replant a tree, but replacing a forest of ancient trees 250–350 years old takes a very long time!

The Blackwood River is the longest permanent waterway in south-western Australia and runs through a deep, winding valley in the hills of the southern Darling Range. The Blackwood is well stocked with marron and trout, and offers year-round canoeing. There are some stunning scenic drives that follow the serpentine course of the river, among the most beautiful hill country in the State. The valley also has excellent bushwalks and is dotted with towns full of character. The Blackwood is a centre for arts, crafts and cultural events like the Bridgetown Blues Festival and the Boyup Brook

The delicate white flowers of clematis (*Clematis pubescens*)
and the yellow flowering waterbush (*Bossiaea aquifolium*)
add splashes of colour to the karri forest in springtime.

Country Music Festival. The valley has a real sense of romance and history, and to me is one of the most interesting areas in inland Western Australia.

The gateway to the valley from the north is the tiny historic settlement of **Mullalyup**, 235 kilometres south of Perth. The Blackwood Inn, now registered on the National Estate, was built as a staging post beside the highway here in 1864. It still offers accommodation and meals. **Balingup** is the next small town, situated in the beautiful Balingup Brook valley surrounded by rolling hills and often blanketed by low mists in winter. Every season offers something special here, with wildflowers in spring, the warm lazy days of summer and the colours of the village's many oak trees in autumn. Balingup is an arts and craft centre, and many creative people live in the area. The Balingup Cheese Factory, originally built

in 1934, has been converted into the Old Cheese Factory Craft Centre, reputed to be the largest in the State. Balingup stages a medieval and tulip festival in spring, and has the reputation of being a 'new age' town, with interesting shops selling natural therapies and herbs. The Bibbulmun Track also passes through the town centre.

Greenbushes, another historic town in the district, had a population of 3,000 in its heyday at the turn of the century, with eight hotels and thirty-four shops. David Stinton discovered tin here in 1888, and the high price of the metal between 1897 and 1910 resulted in the development of a large, vibrant town. Since then, Greenbushes has gradually contracted and today has a population of only 400. The tin and tantalum mine still operates, with a tourist viewing platform over a large open cut, and

Quiet pools on the Blackwood River in summer, which turn into
rapids and fast-flowing waters in winter.

ABOVE Early morning outside a Bibbulmun Track hut, high above the Blackwood River valley.

RIGHT A cheeky rufous tree creeper in a South West forest picnic area.

OVER PAGE Winter mists in the Blackwood River valley at dawn.

there is a small timber mill in the area. The town may be destined to slowly fade away, although there is tourism potential in its rich history. Greenbushes has an Eco-Cultural Discovery Centre, historic buildings and some interesting relics of a bygone age, such as a rough gaol and obsolete mining equipment.

Boyup Brook, the eastern gateway to the Blackwood River valley, is the centre of a fertile sheep, cattle, grain and wine-producing region. The Blackwood River valley wine region has 200 hectares of vines planted and more than thirty individual wineries. The town's main claim to fame is as the venue for the Western Australian Country Music Awards, which are part of the Boyup Brook Country Music Festival, one of the biggest festivals of its type in Australia.

Bridgetown is the major centre of the Blackwood River valley and was originally gazetted as a town site in 1868. The area was first settled by John Blechynden, who selected a 10,000 acre (4,050 hectare) pastoral lease on the Blackwood River in 1857, and Edward Hester, who settled just north of the river in 1858. Blechynden was actually born in the colony, at Perth in 1833. He married his bride, Elizabeth, in 1860, and together they built the magnificent house and gardens of 'Bridgedale' on the Blackwood River, completed in 1862. Today 'Bridgedale' is owned by the National Trust of Australia and is open to the public. Other historic buildings in Bridgetown include the Post Office, the Old Gaol and Police Quarters, and St Paul's Anglican and St Brigid's Catholic churches.

Bridgetown, pictured just after a shower of rain, is the major centre of the Blackwood River valley.

Bridgetown has grown into a busy and attractive town. Situated in the deep, cool valleys of the Blackwood River and Geegelup Brook, it is famous for its low minimum temperatures, consistently among the coldest in the State. The town often has frosty nights, with temperatures below zero in winter. Bridgetown is quite progressive, with its traditional agriculture and timber industries being complemented by new attractions and activities. In November, the town hosts a three-day blues festival, which attracts thousands of visitors and international and local musicians. For one day during the festival, the main street is closed to traffic and hosts a street party with live music, stalls, food and drink, and much revelry. The Blackwood River is a venue for water sports all year round and hosts the longest power dinghy race in the world, the 'Blackwood Classic 250' from Bridgetown to Augusta, and the Blackwood River Marathon, a team event that combines running, cycling, canoeing, swimming and horse riding.

Nannup is also situated on the Blackwood, further to the west, where the river leaves the hills country behind and starts to wind across the Donnybrook sunklands towards Augusta. Nannup is another picturesque small town and has been closely associated with the timber industry throughout its history. Today it offers trout and marron fishing, canoeing, bushwalking and cottage industries like woodworking and other crafts.

One of the largest towns in the tall forests region is **Manjimup**, 309 kilometres south of Perth, with a population of 5,000 people. The word 'manjin' is an Aboriginal name for an edible reed that used to grow in a small swamp near the old town site. Manjimup is the commercial centre of the district and an important timber milling town. The surrounding farmlands have rich, red karri loam soils and support dairy cattle and sheep farms, as well as producing much of Western Australia's potato, onion and cauliflower crop. There are fruit orchards here, too, growing pears, kiwi fruit and many varieties of apple.

Manjimup was settled relatively recently. The town site was not gazetted until 1910, although some hardy pioneers had had pastoral leases in the region before then. The construction of the railway in 1911 was the catalyst for the opening up of this forest wilderness. The mighty trees were felled by hand axe in those days, and then transported by bullock wagon or small locomotives to the timber mill. A Group Settlement Scheme was started in the region in the 1920s, which brought new migrant settlers to clear and farm the land. This had only limited success, however, with many people leaving during the Depression in the 1930s. Much of the land was taken up again by ex-servicemen and their families after World War II.

There are still many forest areas near Manjimup, generally dominated by karri trees or comprising a mix of karri, marri and jarrah. Some of the beauty spots are Fontys Pool, a dammed stream popular for swimming and picnics, the Diamond Tree lookout, a 51 metre high fire observation platform on a karri tree, the 600 year old 'King Jarrah' tree, and the Four Aces, giant 300–400 year old karri trees between 67 and 79 metres high, standing in Indian file. In the town itself is the Manjimup Timber Park, a timber and steam museum with arts and crafts, a blacksmith and a historic hamlet. A major attraction planned for the area is a 'sky-jetty', to be constructed in the deeply incised Donnelly River valley between Manjimup and Nannup. This will offer visitors a gradual climb up through the karri forest canopy, as the valley drops away below, to reach a spectacular view of the valley. It is hoped that the sky-jetty will rival the Tree Top Walk near Walpole in popularity.

Between Manjimup and Pemberton is the interesting Founders Forest (formerly called the 100 Year Forest), which was clearfelled in the 1860s for

Merino sheep above the mist-filled Blackwood River valley.

wheat-growing. The project was abandoned in 1867, and a bushfire in 1875 allowed regeneration of the karri forest. Today it is again a beautiful forest, with stands of 60 metre tall karri trees. The trees have almost reached their full height, but their boles are small and will take another 100 years or so to mature. The Founders Forest shows that karri does regenerate well after logging, but to me it has the feel of a plantation, without the wild, unruly majesty of an old growth forest. The trees are all the same age, marri is almost completely absent and there are no huge old karris.

One feature of virgin forests is that although the majority of the trees are large and old, there is a mix of ages. When one ancient giant dies, or is blown over in a storm, its place is taken by seven or eight saplings that fight to fill the small gap created in the forest canopy. The fallen tree provides a home for moss and lichen, and for forest creatures from termites to marsupials. The wood is gradually broken down by insects, fungi and bacteria and its nutrients are returned to the soil, to be taken up again by surrounding plants. Fire is also an important agent of regeneration in our South West forests; it clears the dense understorey, breaks open the hard seed cases of eucalypts, banksias and other native plants, and creates a fertile ash bed in which these seeds may germinate.

In this way, the forest regenerates in a constant cycle of renewal. There is no such thing as a forest that 'requires' logging to allow regeneration. Timber harvesting is an important industry, but preserving

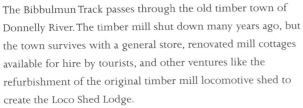

The Bibbulmun Track passes through the old timber town of Donnelly River. The timber mill shut down many years ago, but the town survives with a general store, renovated mill cottages available for hire by tourists, and other ventures like the refurbishment of the original timber mill locomotive shed to create the Loco Shed Lodge.

Neatly kept historic timber mill cottages in Pemberton.

examples of our magnificent original forests is crucial, too, for their biodiversity, beauty and intrinsic worth. In my opinion, these forests have far greater monetary and spiritual value standing than they do as woodchips and sawn logs. The remaining old growth forests in the South West are now protected in national parks, and so they belong to all Australians.

Pemberton is another major centre of the region, and is renowned for its beautiful location and special ambience. The town is situated 342 kilometres south of Perth in the valley of the Lefroy Brook, amid lush, rolling hills and karri trees. It has excellent arts and craft outlets and numerous restaurants, and there are marron and rainbow trout farms, wineries and a large choice of accommodation options in the area.

Horse riding and bushwalking are popular here, and the Bibbulmun Track passes through the town centre.

The Bibelmen Nyoongars were the original custodians of the Pemberton and Northcliffe area. Bibelmen means 'the people who live from the breast', and the country here is rich and plentiful. The first European settlers were Edward Brockman, who settled near the Warren River in 1861, and Pemberton Walcott, who arrived in 1862. Pemberton township was founded in 1913, with the establishment of a timber sawmill. The town is surrounded by forests: the Pemberton Forest Park to the north and the Gloucester National Park to the south.

In the town itself is the historic Pemberton Pool, constructed in 1928. Surrounded by towering karri trees, this is still a lovely place to swim. The Big Brook

Dam, just north of the town, is another popular swimming spot, and is also used for fishing, canoeing and sailboarding. About 4 kilometres south of the town in the Gloucester National Park are the Cascades, a series of small waterfalls on the Lefroy Brook. This is a beautiful spot for a picnic and a wander, especially in winter and spring, when rains have swelled the brook. The Pemberton Tramway has one of its stops at the Cascades on its 36 kilometre journey to Northcliffe, and visitors can alight and enjoy the grandeur of the forest and river. This scenic tramway line is a popular tourist attraction. A steam train also operates from Pemberton to Lyall, near Manjimup, during the cooler months of the year.

Only five minutes from the town centre is one of the area's major attractions, the Gloucester Tree. With a viewing platform 61 metres above the ground, the Gloucester Tree is one of the highest fire lookout trees in the world. It was named after the Duke of Gloucester, who visited the area during the platform's construction in 1946. I have climbed the tree several times, and I must say that my first ascent was nerve-racking. I had climbed up to and around the first corner, when a friend asked me to look down for a photograph. I remember seeing the ground far below between my feet, and my heart skipped a beat. I continued climbing, with sweat pouring from my brow and my hands fiercely gripping the bars. The

Climbing the famous Gloucester Tree near Pemberton can be one of the highlights of a tour of the South West, although it is certainly not for everyone!

ABOVE Dawn reflections on the Warren River, surrounded by dense, virgin karri forest.

OVER PAGE The early morning sun disturbs mists on the Warren River, dawn.

The impressive Hollow Butt karri tree, in the community-managed Northcliffe Forest Park.

tree started to sway, especially towards the top, which certainly did not help my confidence. However, the view from the platform was well worth the effort, with the forest canopy stretching away in all directions.

The other major climbing tree in the Pemberton area is the Dave Evans Bicentennial Tree in Warren National Park, with a platform even higher than the Gloucester, at 68 metres. Warren National Park is a magnificent area of virgin karri forest cloaking the valley of the tranquil Warren River. There are some good bushwalks here and three excellent campsites on the river banks. This national park, with a one-way scenic drive and lookouts over the river, is one of the best areas in which to view the towering karri forests. Another conservation area near Pemberton is the Beedelup National Park, which also boasts old growth karri forests as well as the Beedelup Falls, a series of cascades over granite rocks with a total fall of

106 metres. There is a 300 metre walk trail here, with a suspension bridge over the falls, which are at their best in winter and spring. Beedelup National Park has recently increased in size from just 1,710 hectares to more than 18,460 hectares, with the inclusion of further areas of old growth forest.

The Warren valley is Western Australia's newest wine-producing area. There are more than fifty vineyards and more than 500 hectares of vines planted, and wine varieties include Cabernet Sauvignon, Chardonnay, Pinot Noir and Shiraz. The first trial plantings were in 1982, but the majority of the vineyards have been established only in the last decade. The district already looks as though it will become one of the finest wine areas in the State. Many of the rivers and streams in the area, such as the Warren, Donnelly and Gardner, offer excellent canoeing and inland fishing. They are stocked annually with rainbow and brown trout fingerlings from the

Pemberton Trout Hatchery. Marron are also caught in the region's rivers but only in a strictly controlled, short fishing season that opens in the summer months.

Near the southern margin of the tall forests is the small town of **Northcliffe**, nestled in among giant karri and marri trees. In common with many of the other towns in the region, Northcliffe has diversified its economic base, with tourism a fast-growing industry. Many new national parks have recently been proclaimed in the forests near Northcliffe, such as the Boorara and Jane national parks. Four-wheel-drive tours are available from here or from Pemberton to the wild southern coastline or to

The Cascades near Pemberton, on the Lefroy Brook, are a great place for a picnic and a stroll around, with beautiful forest and river scenery.

places like the spectacular Yeagarup Dunes, mountains of sand that are slowly moving inland, swallowing trees and lakes as they go.

Next to the town itself is the Northcliffe Forest Park, a beautiful area of relatively undisturbed karri, marri and jarrah forest leading down to the Gardner River. There are two picnic spots here and some good bushwalking trails (see appendix). The Bibbulmun Track passes through Northcliffe, which enables long-distance walkers to replenish their food stocks or perhaps have a night of luxury in a caravan park or hotel. About 17 kilometres to the east of the town is another of the beauty spots of the area, Lane Poole Falls, accessed by a 5 kilometre return bushwalk through the Boorara National Park (see appendix).

Further east again is the Shannon National Park, 53 kilometres south of Manjimup. This superb national park protects virtually all of the Shannon River catchment, which drains water from the forests into the pristine, tannin-stained waters of Broke Inlet. The park was declared in 1988, after large sections of the forest had been logged, but remains

ABOVE Looking up the incredibly smooth, ivory trunks of towering karri trees in the Warren National Park.
OPPOSITE Giant karri trees in the Warren National Park in autumn, with their new salmon pink bark.

ABOVE One of the lesser known but spectacular attractions of the Pemberton area is the Yeagarup Dunes, near the south coast.

OPPOSITE The spectacular Beedelup Falls near Pemberton, seen at their best in winter and spring.

an important reserve because it preserves an entire river ecosystem. The national park is 53,500 hectares in size, with mixed karri, jarrah and marri forests leading down to the heaths and wetlands of the coastal areas. There are some areas of magnificent old growth forest, which can be seen on the Great Forest Trees Drive, a 48 kilometre circuit along gravel roads. The drive leads to lookouts and boardwalks in the forest, and there are many picnic areas along its route. It even has its own radio transmitters providing a commentary about the vegetation and animals of the park, which include quokkas, quendas, mardos and western grey kangaroos. Bushwalking is another popular activity, with excellent tracks like the

Great Forest Trees Walk and Mokares Rock walk trail (see appendix).

The Shannon National Park has a camping area located on the site of the once-thriving Shannon town. A timber mill, at one stage the largest in the State, used to operate here. It closed in 1968, and there are few reminders of its existence, except for the cleared area of the camping ground with its exotic pine trees.

South of Northcliffe, the tall forests sweep down towards the sea, gradually giving way to stunted jarrah and marri mallees, and then to coastal heathlands with pockets of banksia and peppermint woodlands. The heathland areas are rich in wildflower species,

PREVIOUS SPREAD The beautiful Salmon Beach near Point D'Entrecasteaux and Windy Harbour is a popular fishing spot.
RIGHT Wild surf set against limestone cliffs at Point D'Entrecasteaux.
OPPOSITE View east from the granite dome of Mt Chudalup, 188 metres above sea level.

with a colourful display from September to November. Occasional granite domes rise above the surrounding countryside, like the impressive 188 metre high Mt Chudalup, which you pass on the way to Point D'Entrecasteaux. There is a picnic area here and a walk track to the summit (see appendix). This area is protected within the enormous D'Entrecasteaux National Park (115,787 hectares), which stretches along the coast from near Augusta to connect with the Shannon and Walpole-Nornalup national parks in the east. In the 160 kilometre long wilderness coastline between Augusta and Mandalay Beach near Walpole, there is only one two-wheel-drive access road to the coast, which leads to the small settlement of **Windy Harbour**. This cluster of shacks, tucked in behind the imposing limestone headland of Point D'Entrecasteaux, is well named: there is no shortage of breezes for most of the year. It is a wonderful, relaxing spot, with good fishing and protected swimming beaches.

A road from Windy Harbour heads a short distance west to Salmon Beach, with its crashing waves and white sands enclosed in a wall of high limestone cliffs. It is one of the most magnificent spots I have ever encountered. Salmon Beach has excellent swimming, surfing and fishing. Another recently built road leads from near the beach up to the unmanned lighthouse at Point D'Entrecasteaux. There are a series of walk trails here that wind through low coastal heath and unusual rock formations to lookout points above the awesome limestone cliffs. Walkers must stick to the paths and take care, as the cliffs are dangerously unstable and the weather can often be windy and bleak. The rest of the vast expanse of the D'Entrecasteaux National Park is mainly a wilderness area, but there are a few four-wheel-drive tracks that can be followed to pristine fishing beaches, wetlands, river mouths and imposing headlands.

The tall forests region has a wealth of attractions for visitors, with the natural landscapes here the most compelling. I have happy memories of walking the Bibbulmun Track in the Blackwood River valley, of wandering, awed, through misty giant karri trees at dawn near the Warren River, and of fishing for salmon on an untouched beach on the south coast. I managed to catch one (I am not a great fisherman, by any stretch of the imagination), and I remember gazing up and down the smooth sweep of beach, with not a trace of human 'progress' visible, and thinking how lucky I was to live in this part of the world.

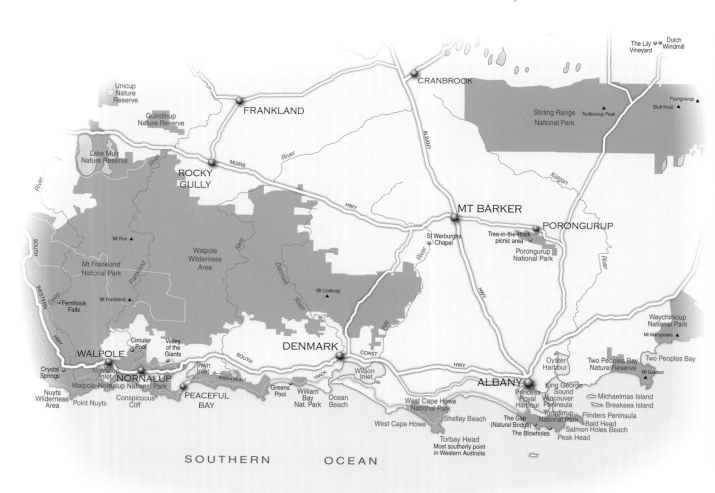

The Great Southern

This region covers the southernmost portion of Western Australia, extending east along the coast from Walpole to Mt Manypeaks, and inland to the Porongurup and Stirling ranges. The area is renowned for its beauty and scenic diversity.

The Lily   Dutch
Vineyard   Windmill

CRANBROOK

Unicup
Nature
Reserve

Pyungoorup
Bluff Knoll

Quindinup
Nature Reserve

FRANKLAND

Stirling Range
National Park

Toolbrunup Peak

Lake Muir
Nature Reserve

River

MUIRS

River

ROCKY
GULLY

ALBANY

Kalgan

HWY

MT BARKER

PORONGURUP

Mt Roe

Walpole
Wilderness
Area

Kent

St Werburghs
Chapel

Tree-in-the-Rock
picnic area

Porongurup
National Park

River

Mt Frankland
National Park

Denmark

Mt Lindesay

HWY

River

WESTERN

Deep

SOUTH

Mt Frankland

River

Waychinicup
National Park

Fernhook
Falls

Mt Manypeaks

HWY

Circular
Pool

Valley
of the
Giants

DENMARK

COAST

WALPOLE

SOUTH

Wilson
Inlet

HWY

Oyster
Harbour

Two Peoples Bay
Nature Reserve

Two Peoples Bay

Crystal
Springs

Nornalup
Inlet

NORNALUP

Irwin
Inlet

BIBBULMUN

TRACK

Greens
Pool

William
Bay
Nat. Park

Ocean
Beach

ALBANY

Princess
Royal
Harbour

King George
Sound

Vancouver
Peninsula

Mt Gardner

Michaelmas Island

Nuyts
Wilderness
Area

Point Nuyts

Conspicuous
Cliff

Walpole-Nornalup National Park

PEACEFUL
BAY

West Cape Howe
National Park

Shelley Beach

The Gap
(Natural Bridge)

The Blowholes

Torndirrup
National Park

Peak Head

Bald Head

Salmon Holes Beach

Breaksea Island

Flinders Peninsula

West Cape Howe

Torbay Head
Most southerly point
in Western Australia

SOUTHERN   OCEAN

N

0   20km

Chapter 4

THE GREAT SOUTHERN

The southernmost area of Western Australia is a microcosm of the scenic wonders of the world. Few places offer so much in such a small geographical area. There are lush forests of giant trees, superb beaches with crisp, clean sand, coastal cliffs and dramatic coastal formations, inlets and estuaries, and genuine mountain scenery in the Stirling and Porongurup ranges. These peaks even have occasional snowfalls in winter, although skiing is not recommended! The Great Southern is a popular nature-based tourist destination and is justifiably famous for its beautiful and well-preserved natural environments. To complement this, there are fertile farming areas, historic centres like Albany and award-winning wineries.

The region begins at **Walpole**, where the tall forest of the South West meets the sea. This is a luxuriant area, with rivers meandering through forested hills, inlets teeming with marine life, and magnificent forests of karri and tingle extending down to the water's edge. The town of Walpole lies on the Walpole and Nornalup inlets, and excellent cruises are available to the mouth of the sea and to secluded beaches. Nornalup Inlet was used as a harbour by sealing and whaling ships in the early 1800s, even before the settlement at Albany was established. The first European settlers on the inlet were George Bellanger, a French lawyer, and the Thompson family, who arrived in 1911. Walpole itself was not established until the 1930s, when a land settlement scheme began in the area for families hit by the Depression.

The townships of Walpole and Nornalup are almost completely surrounded by the 18,166 hectare Walpole-Nornalup National Park. The park protects the southern coastline and encompasses coastal heathlands, woodlands of peppermint and banksia trees, tall forests and many inland waterways. The animal life includes western grey kangaroos, quokkas, and pygmy, ringtail and brushtail possums. There are about 110 species of bird present. The area is drenched with more than 1,400 millimetres of rain a year, making it one of the wettest and least seasonal parts of the State.

There are three species of eucalypt growing within a 10 kilometre radius of Walpole that are endemic to the region: the red tingle (*Eucalyptus jacksonii*), the yellow tingle (*E. guilfoylei*) and the Rates tingle (*E. brevistylis*). All of the tingle species are huge, but the red tingle gives the Valley of the Giants its name. These massive trees grow to about 70 metres in height and can have a circumference of 20 metres. Their spreading, buttressed trunks are often hollowed out by repeated fires, and some ancient giants of the forest cling to life through only a few small remaining sections of living bark at their base, which somehow support the height

PREVIOUS SPREAD In among some of the largest living things on Earth—red tingle trees, near Walpole.

ABOVE This red tingle tree, near Hilltop Road, is reputed to be the largest buttressed eucalypt in the world.

and weight of the tree. The tingle species usually grow in association with karri, and the forests have a dense understorey of karri hazel, karri wattle, cutleaf hibbertia, tree hovea and umbrella plants. In a past, wetter era, both tingle and karri used to be much more widespread in the South West but they have contracted to their present ranges as the climate has become gradually hotter and drier.

The Valley of the Giants is one of the most famous attractions of the area. The valley is 22 kilometres east of Walpole and includes the remarkable Tree Top Walk, a 600 metre loop walkway through the forest canopy. As you walk out onto lightweight metal bridges, supported by pylons, the ground drops away below. The walkway is some 40 metres above the ground at its highest point. From here, it is easy to appreciate the size and majesty of the giant tingle

and karri trees. The treetops abound with birds and the views are excellent. The walkway is suitable for assisted wheelchairs, but those who have a fear of heights should be aware that it sways in windy conditions.

The other main attraction at the Valley of the Giants is a boardwalk through the Ancient Empire, a grove of enormous and very old red tingle trees. Some of these trees are 500 years old, and many have huge trunk hollows that you can stand in or actually walk through. At the Ancient Empire, take a moment to admire the beautiful grey textured bark of the tingles, the strange shapes like human faces in the tree trunks, and the stillness of this timeless forest.

Walpole has many other attractions and activities, with the Walpole and Nornalup inlets famous for their fishing, sailing and boating. The Frankland River

ABOVE Red flowering gum (*Corymbia ficifolia*) near Walpole, January.

OVER PAGE The popular Tree Top Walk through the tingle and karri forest canopy, in the Valley of the Giants.

feeds into the Nornalup Inlet and is popular with canoeists and picnickers. There are a number of excellent bushwalking areas near Walpole. A short heritage trail (2 kilometres one way) leads from the town's tourist centre to Coalmine Beach and the Knoll, with interpretive signs and historical informa- tion. This trail is part of the Bibbulmun Track, which also passes through the Valley of the Giants on its way along the south coast to Albany.

In 2001, four new national parks were proclaimed in the Walpole area to form the largest expanse of wilderness in the South West. The Walpole Wilderness Area stretches from the South Western Highway to east of Mt Lindesay, near Denmark, and extends from the south coast inland to the Muirs Highway. In all, it covers an area of 360,000 hectares, with virgin forests of karri, jarrah and tingle trees and occasional granite peaks piercing their green expanse. There are also coastal heathlands, wetland areas and stunning wild rivers such as the Frankland. The area has much in common with the famous south-west wilderness area of Tasmania.

One of the most beautiful parts of the wilderness area (and indeed in the South West) is Mt Frankland, some 29 kilometres north of Walpole. The area is well worth a visit, with a small camping area and a number of walk trails, including one to the top of the 422 metre high peak (see appendix). The region has several other excellent camping areas, such as those at Fernhook Falls on the Deep River and Crystal Springs on the South Western Highway. There are plans for a karri-tingle discovery centre and outdoor classroom in the wilderness area, along with other ecotourism initiatives.

A short distance east of Walpole is the small township of **Nornalup**, on the banks of the Frankland River. Near Nornalup, a gravel road heads south to the prominent coastal formation of Conspicuous Cliff. A walkway and staircase here climb to a viewing point, which overlooks a stunning beach and imposing limestone headland. This is a good spot to look for southern right whales during the season from August to October. The beach, which offers good fishing and surfing, can be reached via another walkway. Ficifolia Road heads east from Conspicuous Cliff to the popular coastal resort town of **Peaceful Bay**, passing through stands of the endemic red flowering gum (*Corymbia ficifolia*), which put on a spectacular display in January.

William Bay National Park, 14 kilometres west of Denmark, is situated on one of the most beautiful stretches of coastline in Australia, with protected lagoons, cool, clear waters and brilliant white sandy beaches. In a short distance of about 3 kilometres are four separate and very different beaches for visitors to savour. The first reached by the access road is Greens Pool. The pool has inviting waters of emerald and turquoise protected by a circle of small granite islands, and is safe for swimming and snorkelling. Just around a headland is the next tiny bay, where huge grey granite boulders scarred with deep cracks and fissures emerge from ivory sands. This is the appropriately named Elephant Rocks beach, with a herd of stone 'elephants' enjoying a dip in the sea.

Madfish Bay is next, with twin lagoons protected by an outlying granite reef. Finally, we discover Waterfall Beach, which has a freshwater stream and a small waterfall that cascades directly onto the sandy beach. William Bay National Park also protects heathlands and patches of karri forest.

Denmark, situated on the Denmark River and the large Wilson Inlet, 414 kilometres south of Perth, is one of the most picturesque towns in Western Australia. The area is hilly, with some excellent scenic drives through forests to lookouts and beaches. The Mt Shadforth Drive along the top of the Bennett Range is one of the best, providing some extensive views. The ground drops steeply from the hilltops to deep green pastures and karri forests, with Wilson Inlet and the ocean in the distance. If you turn to the north, etched on the skyline is Mt Lindesay, the highest peak in the Denmark area, with the jagged Stirling and Porongurup ranges in the distance. Mt Lindesay has a picnic area and ascent track (see appendix). The drive can be made into a circuit by returning along Scotsdale Road, another scenic route through forest and farmland. There is also a drive along the shores of Wilson Inlet to Ocean Beach, which offers swimming, surfing and fishing. It is often a good place to catch salmon between February and April.

The Denmark area was first explored by Europeans when naval surgeon Dr Thomas Wilson from the Albany settlement discovered the Denmark River and climbed Mt Lindesay in 1829. The town of Denmark was not established until 1895, when a timber industry began in the area. The Millar brothers opened a mill, which was successful for ten years. When all the accessible karri was logged, the mill closed and the town struggled on until thousands

PREVIOUS SPREAD Sunset hour at Coalmine Beach and the Knoll, near Walpole.
OPPOSITE TOP Rapids in the Frankland River near Circular Pool.
OPPOSITE BOTTOM Springtime wildflowers and bright new leaves at Mt Frankland, October.

of migrants arrived after World War I as part of the Group Settlement Scheme. The Depression of the 1930s hit Denmark hard, and destitute people left the land in droves. Today, however, Denmark is a thriving town, with an interesting mix of agricultural pursuits, from emu and marron farms to orchards, traditional sheep and cattle properties and wineries. There are numerous restaurants and cafes, and a large choice of accommodation is available in this growing tourist region. Denmark also is home to many talented artisans and craftspeople.

Some 160 species of bird are found in the region, with Wilson Inlet being an important feeding ground for many migratory wader species. You might also see ospreys, along with splendid and redwing fairy wrens and many species of parrot. The main karri belt ends near Denmark; further east, there are only small relict patches at places like the Porongurups and Mt Manypeaks. Other forest trees around Denmark include jarrah, marri, yellow tingle, bullich, yate and blackbutt. The understorey of these forests can be very colourful in spring, with species of *Beaufortia*, *Hovea*, *Boronia* and *Clematis*.

The southernmost point in Western Australia, Torbay Head, is located in West Cape Howe National Park, some 38 kilometres east of Denmark. West Cape Howe

BELOW The colourful coral vine (*Kennedia coccinea*), Mt Frankland, October.

OPPOSITE TOP Elephant Rocks, William Bay National Park.
OPPOSITE BOTTOM View from Mt Shadforth Drive near Denmark, over lush farmland and karri trees to Wilson Inlet in the distance.

A mystical dawn at Mt Frankland, with mist below the peak and high clouds obscuring the sun.

is a starkly beautiful place of dramatic, black dolerite cliffs, pristine beaches and heath-covered headlands. There are small swamp areas and patches of karri forest, with the trees as large in diameter and as old as those further west but only about half the height. Most of West Cape Howe is a wilderness area accessible only by four-wheel-drive vehicle or on foot. The exception is the camping site, accessible by two-wheel-drive vehicle, at Shelley Beach, located between steep limestone headlands, and with its own freshwater stream emanating from a deep valley in the hills. The national park is a mecca for adventure enthusiasts, with excellent bushwalking, hang-gliding and rock climbing available. The Bibbulmun Track traverses the park, and it is also possible to walk from Shelley Beach to the cliffs of West Cape Howe (see appendix).

Hang-gliders use a lookout point above Shelley Beach and take advantage of the easterly winds of summer and the fact that there is a smooth, wide beach to land on below the takeoff points. Some expert hang-gliding enthusiasts can stay in the air for a number of hours, soaring in the updrafts created by the onshore breeze. The igneous, dolerite cliffs of West Cape Howe are a rock climber's paradise, offering many difficult and challenging climbs. This area provides some of the best climbing in Australia, with the black, gothic rocks and the crashing waves creating an atmosphere all its own. The precipice margins are similar to a moonscape landscape, with

The black dolerite cliffs of West Cape Howe are a popular rock climbing area.

Shelley Beach, in West Cape Howe National Park, offers camping next to a freshwater stream and good fishing, and is also popular with hang-gliding enthusiasts.

Much of the south coast is rugged, with dramatic cliffs and rocky headlands covered in wildflower-rich coastal heaths.

scattered rock fragments and very little vegetation. West Cape Howe has a chasm in the rocks, formed by the pounding Southern Ocean, that is almost twice the height and size of the more famous 'Gap' near Albany.

Albany, founded in 1826, three years before the Swan River settlement, is the oldest town in Western Australia. It is cradled between the twin hills of Melville and Clarence on the beautiful natural anchorages of Princess Royal Harbour and King George Sound. The town has a historic charm and is nostalgic of the old days of sailing ships and life on the high seas. The weather here is often blustery and overcast, but this seems to suit the town's colonial image. Recently, a wind farm was completed on the coastal cliffs 12 kilometres south-west of Albany, to take advantage of these strong winds. The twelve 65 metre high towers, with their 35 metre blades, supply about 75 per cent of Albany's electricity needs and form the largest wind energy project in Australia. Albany does have sunny skies, too, and its annual rainfall is only 930 millimetres, less than that of Margaret River or Pemberton. Probably the best time of year to visit is from March to May, when there are usually clear skies, cool nights and calm seas. The town is 409 kilometres south-east of Perth and has a population of about 28,000.

King George Sound was first discovered by Europeans in 1791, when Captain George Vancouver landed at Frenchman Bay and claimed the coastline for the British Crown. He overlooked the fact that the land was already occupied by the Mineng Nyoongar group, the original custodians of this region. Albany was founded on Boxing Day 1826, when Major Edmund Lockyer, fifty-two convicts and their escorting soldiers established a penal outpost of New South Wales. They called their new settlement Frederickstown after Frederick, the Duke of York and Albany and Earl of Ulster. The town was renamed Albany in 1832 after being proclaimed as part of the Swan River Colony.

The Albany settlement was unusual in colonial Australia for the harmonious relationship between the Mineng Aborigines and the European settlers in the first decade. There was almost no competition for food and resources, the settlers did not impose their values and religious beliefs on the Mineng, and there was no dependence on Aboriginal labour. Within two days of landing at Princess Royal Harbour, Major Lockyer had to deal with a major incident that could have changed all this. He sent a boat to investigate smoke signals on Michaelmas Island, and the landing party discovered a group of four Aboriginal men who had been marooned there by unscrupulous sealers. The Aborigines, some with old cutlass scars, were transported to the mainland, but soon after their release attacked a convict work party, spearing one of the men. However, Lockyer ordered that no reprisal be made. He said:

> on reflecting that these people had made this attack in consequence of the injuries they had received, I gave positive orders that no retaliation should take place on our side except in absolute self defence.*

This enlightened attitude helped to ensure that no further conflicts occurred and allowed good relations to develop at Albany between the two races. In particular, the friendship between Mokare and Dr Alexander Collie was remarkable. Mokare and his brother Nakina often lived with Collie in his house and accompanied him and others like Surgeon Wilson on exploratory expeditions into the interior. When Mokare died in 1831, his grave was dug by European men under the direction of Nakina and other Aboriginal elders. Collie died of tuberculosis

---

*E. Lockyer, 'Journal of Major Lockyer: Commandent [sic] of the Expedition Sent from Sydney in 1826 to Found a Settlement at King George's Sound, Western Australia', 1826.

ABOVE Albany sunset from near the Gap in Torndirrup National Park.

OVER PAGE The beautiful Aldridge Cove in the Nuyts Wilderness Area is accessible only by foot.

four years later and, at his request, was buried alongside his friend Mokare. Unfortunately, the growth of the settlement at Albany eventually reduced the food resources available to the Aborigines and this, along with the effects of disease, led to high mortality rates among the Mineng people and the gradual loss of their traditional way of life.

Albany has a unique blend of history and natural beauty. There are more than fifty buildings of heritage value in the town and a superb coastline of beaches, cliffs and dramatic coastal formations. The colours of Princess Royal Harbour and King George Sound are spectacular on a clear day, with intense turquoise shallows and navy-blue deep waters. Geologically speaking, the base rocks of the area are ancient Precambrian granites and gneisses, from 1,200 to 1,600 million years old, overlain in many

places by relatively recently formed limestone derived from sea-shells and sand grains.

The main area of natural attractions near Albany is the Torndirrup National Park on Flinders Peninsula, some 20 kilometres from the town centre. There are many good bushwalks here, as well as famous icons like the Gap, Natural Bridge and the Blowholes. The national park, 3,906 hectares in size, attracts nearly a quarter of a million visitors a year, making it one of the most visited parks in Western Australia. The scenery is dramatic, with the wild Southern Ocean on one side of the peninsula juxtaposed with the calm, sheltered waters of Princess Royal Harbour and King George Sound to the north. The vegetation varies from wildflower-rich heathlands to peppermint woodlands and small areas of medium-height karri and bullich trees.

The 24 metre high cliffs of the Gap, in Torndirrup National Park, are one of Albany's most famous attractions.

Two of the main attractions in the national park are the Gap and Natural Bridge, only about 100 metres apart on the southern coastline. The Gap is a 24 metre deep chasm in the granite, into which massive ocean swells surge and break. A viewing platform above the chasm is often doused with spray from the pounding sea. Natural Bridge is an arc of granite of enormous size, which has been completely undercut by wave action. If you dare, you can even walk onto this rock bridge (at your own risk—and not recommended in high seas!). Nearby are the Blowholes, reached by a walk of 1.6 kilometres return, with a long uphill haul on the way back. I remember well my first visit to the Blowholes on a rough, windy day. When my friends and I reached the site, we could not seem to find these famous holes. All of a sudden, there was an almighty rush of air from fissures in the rock right next to my position high above the sea and I jumped about 3 feet into the air! It sounded very similar to a blast from a steam train running at speed and came as a complete surprise. Needless to say, I would recommend the Blowholes as worth visiting, although they may be less spectacular on a calm day.

Also in the national park are the beautiful spots of Jimmy Newhills Harbour and Salmon Holes Beach. The highest point of the park, Stony Hill, has a 400 metre interpretive circuit, offering views of the coastline and inland to the Stirling and Porongurup ranges. Another lookout over the Southern Ocean is at Sharp Point, with a short trail of 500 metres. The Great Southern region is often called the 'Rainbow Coast'—an apt name because even in summer there can be occasional showers interspersed with periods of sunshine and warmth. The weather is changeable and unpredictable, and winter often brings fierce storms and gale-force winds. Freak 'king waves' and rips are common along this dangerous coast, and people have been swept off rocks and drowned. The power of the ocean must always be respected.

Salmon Holes near Albany is a popular fishing and surfing beach.

Another nature-based tourist attraction at Albany is whale watching. From late July to mid-October, cruises from the port take visitors to watch southern right whales (*Balaena australis*) at play. These huge mammals, up to 18 metres in length and weighing 80 tonnes, migrate to the southern coast of Western Australia to mate, give birth and raise their young. If you are lucky, you might see them leaping out of the water (breaching) or hitting their giant tail flukes on the water (tail lobbing). Every year, more southern right whales return to King George Sound—a pleasing sight, considering that up until recently these waters were used for whaling. The last whaling station in Australia, at Frenchman Bay on Flinders Peninsula, finally closed in 1978. It is now open to visitors as a whaling museum known as Jaycee's Whale World.

Albany has become more cosmopolitan over the years and is shaking off its former image as a rough port and whaling town. The main city centre and York Street have been upgraded to include a cappuccino strip and smart shopping areas, and historical buildings and facades have been restored. Some of the more notable buildings here are the Albany Town Hall, built in 1888, and the Old Albany Post Office, opened in 1870 with a roof of sheoak shingles. This imposing building now houses a restaurant and The University of Western Australia's Albany Centre. The Anglican Church of St John the Evangelist, on York Street, is a beautiful, serene place of worship built of locally quarried granite and was consecrated in 1848.

Near the town centre is the Albany Residency

The Old Albany Post Office, first opened in 1870, now houses a restaurant and The University of Western Australia's Albany Centre.

St John the Evangelist Anglican Church in Albany is one of the oldest in the State (consecrated in 1848) and was built from locally quarried granite.

Museum, and the brig *Amity*, a replica of Major Lockyer's ship, which is located just 200 metres from where the first settlers landed at Point Frederick. The *Amity* is well worth exploring. I was amazed at the cramped and difficult conditions on board: even the captain and first officer cabins are tiny, while the convicts had it far worse, crammed in the hull along with all their provisions and other stores. Another important historical site is the first farm in Western Australia, the Old Farm at Strawberry Hill, which was established to supply food to the Albany settlement. The original home on the property, built in 1831 by Dr Alexander Collie, was destroyed by fire in 1870. The present two-storey building was built in 1836 for Captain Sir Richard Spencer, Albany's first Government Resident. The oldest building in Albany is 'Patrick Taylor Cottage' on Duke Street, built around 1832 of wattle and daub. The cottage is open to visitors and furnished with antiques and period costumes. There are many other buildings of interest in Albany, including the

Old Gaol, built in 1851, and the Vancouver Arts Centre, a historical building now housing an art gallery.

Mt Clarence and Mt Melville both have lookouts that provide sweeping views over the town and the magnificent coastline and harbours. Mt Clarence is the site of the Desert Mounted Corps Memorial, which was originally on the Suez Canal but was moved to Albany in 1964 after being damaged in riots. Just to the east, on a third hill, Mt Adelaide, is the Princess Royal Fortress, Australia's first national fortress, commissioned in 1893 to protect the isolated settlement of Albany and its strategic harbours. A recommended drive from Albany town centre skirts around Mt Clarence and Mt Adelaide and along Marine Drive to Middleton Beach. The scenery is breathtaking, and there are a number of lookouts over Princess Royal Harbour and King George Sound, with Michaelmas and Breaksea islands on the horizon. The beautiful Middleton Beach, sheltered from the heavy ocean swells by Flinders Peninsula, is overlooked by the Grand Esplanade Hotel. The beach offers safe swimming

ABOVE The Old Farm at Strawberry Hill was established in the early days of colonization to supply food for the fledgling King George Sound settlement.

OVER PAGE Little Beach, at Two Peoples Bay, is one of my favourite South West beaches, with white sands washed by the clear waters of the Southern Ocean and surrounded by high granite hills.

if you can brave the cold waters of the Southern Ocean!

Another coastal destination near Albany is Two Peoples Bay, a nature reserve of stunning turquoise coves, granite peaks and coastal heathlands. The name commemorates the meeting here in 1803 of Captain Pendleton of the United States sealing brig *Union* and an exploratory group led by Midshipman Ransonnet of the French ship *Geographe*. They named this beautiful coast 'Baie de Deux Peuples'. Little Beach, in the reserve, is one of my favourite South West beaches.

Two Peoples Bay is a unique area of deeply incised gullies running down from the granite peak of Mt Gardner (400 metres) to the ocean, with small streams

and moist habitats that have not been burnt for a long time. This has enabled the survival of some extremely rare bird and mammal species that have disappeared from other areas of the South West. There have been two remarkable rediscoveries here. The first, the noisy scrub-bird, was originally discovered in 1842 by John Gilbert but had been presumed extinct since the turn of the century. These loud songbirds were once found over most of the South West, but the change in fire regimes and the clearance of habitat with the arrival of Europeans led to their disappearance. However, in 1961 an amateur ornithologist from Albany, Harley Webster, saw an unusual bird with a loud call at Two Peoples Bay. To his surprise, it was identified as a noisy scrub-bird. As a

A New Holland honeyeater in the Porongurup Range.

The mysterious Stirling Range rises abruptly from the seemingly endless plains of the Western Australian Wheatbelt. The peaks here are (left to right): Ellen, Pyungoorup, the Arrows and Isongerup.

Dawn view over farmland to Nancy Peak (652 metres) and Gibraltar Rock (640 metres) in the Porongurup Range.

result of his discovery, the Two Peoples Bay Nature Reserve was proclaimed in 1967 to help protect the species. The original population of 100 birds has increased to more than 1,000, and many have been translocated to other parts of the South West. The area has 188 bird species in all, and also harbours other rare birds such as the western whipbird and western bristlebird.

Two Peoples Bay had another surprise in store. After fox baiting began in the reserve in 1988, many small mammal species started increasing in numbers. Then in late 1994, the officially extinct Gilbert's potoroo was rediscovered on the slopes of Mt Gardner. This small marsupial, also originally discovered by John Gilbert, had not been reliably reported anywhere in the South West for more than 100 years. It remains very rare in the reserve, although the elimination of foxes has allowed a gradual increase in the population.

The Great Southern region is also renowned for the beauty of its hinterland. The main inland town is **Mt Barker**, situated under a hill of the same name that was ascended by Dr Thomas Wilson in 1829 with the Aboriginal guide Mokare. His comment on the area was: 'a country beautifully diversified by moderately elevated hills and fertile verdant valleys adorned and enriched by streams of the purest water'.* Pioneering settlers soon arrived in the 1830s, and the town is now an important centre for the surrounding agricultural industry. The Great Southern hinterland is a fertile farming area, with predominantly wheat, sheep and cattle properties. A recent growth industry is plantations of blue gums for the export woodchip market.

*Quoted in J. Cross, ed., *Journal of Several Expeditions Made in W.A. during the Years 1829, 30, 31, 32*, facsimile edn, University of Western Australia Press, Nedlands, 1980.

TOP The magnificent Queen of Sheba orchid (*Thelymitra variegata*), one of the most beautiful but elusive wildflowers of the South West, is seen here in the Stirling Range.
BOTTOM Lush marri and karri forest near Hayward Peak in the Porongurups.

Another relatively new, but important, industry is viticulture. The first Riesling and Cabernet Sauvignon grapes were trialed near Mt Barker in 1967, with excellent results. There are now more than 800 hectares of vineyards around Mt Barker, Frankland, Denmark and the Porongurup Range. The region is renowned for its top-quality table wines. Riesling is the most famous varietal, and other excellent wines are produced from Chardonnay, Cabernet Sauvignon and Shiraz grapes. Many of the wineries offer tastings and sales, often in beautiful rural settings.

Mt Barker is the gateway to the majestic Stirling and Porongurup ranges, the only real mountains in the southern half of Western Australia. Both ranges are protected by national parks and are areas of rugged beauty, unspoilt wilderness environments and many outdoor activities. Offering quiet and peaceful retreats from the bustle of the modern world, the mountains are popular with bushwalkers, rock climbers, wildflower enthusiasts and naturalists.

The Porongurup Range rises to 670 metres above sea level at its highest point, Devils Slide, and is only 48 kilometres north of Albany. The hills are cloaked in a verdant forest of karri trees, which has been isolated from the main karri belt for at least 5,000 years. There are also jarrah and marri forests on the lower slopes and granite vegetation communities on the peaks of the range. The mountains here, such as Gibraltar Rock and the Twin Peaks, are impressive, with their sheer granite walls rising far above the mighty karri trees in the valleys. The granite was formed in the Precambrian period about 1,100 million years ago, making the range one of the oldest in the world. The Porongurups offer some of the best bushwalking in the South West, with lush and varied vegetation, challenging climbs and panoramic views. Some of the popular walks are detailed in the appendix.

The Stirling Range National Park protects an outstanding wilderness area of 115,661 hectares, which contains within its boundaries more than 1,500 plant species, eighty-two of them found nowhere else in the world. Probably the most famous of the endemic species are the beautiful *Darwinia* mountain bells, with nine species confined to specific small areas of the park. The springtime wildflower display in the Stirlings, from August to November, is magnificent, with abundant orchids, banksias, hakeas, isopogons and bottlebrushes. The mountains also have a wealth of animal life, with some endemic species like the palisade spider, and mammals like the western grey kangaroo, honey possum, pygmy possum and quenda.

Bull banksia (*Banksia grandis*) and coral vine (*Kennedia coccinea*), Porongurup Range. Banksias are among the most spectacular plants of the South West, with fifty-nine of the worldwide total of seventy-six species endemic in the region.

Early morning view from Bluff Knoll, with Toolbrunup (left) and Mt Trio in the distance, rising above a sea of cloud, Stirling Range.

The Stirling Range is a hiking paradise (see appendix) and offers many other adventure activities such as rock climbing, abseiling and gliding. The rugged sandstone and quartzite peaks were originally sediments deposited in a shallow inland sea, which have been subsequently uplifted and eroded during the last 100 million years to form the mountains. Even today, you can find ripple rocks on top of the peaks, evidence of the marine origin of the sediments. Bluff Knoll (1,095 metres) is the highest peak in the range, followed closely by Pyungoorup (1,060 metres) and Toolbrunup (1,052 metres). The Stirling Range has the distinction of being the only place in Western Australia that has snow every year, although the falls are usually very light. Occasionally, falls of more than 5 centimetres occur, and people come from all over the South West to climb Bluff Knoll,

play in the snow and delight in what is an unusual experience for this part of the world.

The Great Southern is truly a magnificent region. In many ways, it is characteristic of the South West as a whole, with an abundance of natural beauty and infinite variety. It is a privilege to travel through and photograph these awe-inspiring areas, and, even though I live and work in Perth, I must admit that my heart often yearns to be 'down south' on an adventure. Maybe some day I will move down to the forests or the coast, and finally discover all the secrets of the South West—if that is possible! I hope that we are able to take care of this priceless natural heritage so that future generations will be able to enjoy, as much as I have, the wild surf shores, untrammelled forests and ancient hills of the South West.

APPENDIX

BUSHWALKS OF THE SOUTH WEST

It is not my intention to describe all the bushwalks of the South West in detail, rather to provide an overview of the best and most popular tracks in the region. The walks presented here pass through spectacular natural environments and some of the most beautiful scenic areas in the South West. I recommend sampling a few of them between wineries! I have graded the walks as follows:

Grade 1: Easy, short walk; good path.
Grade 2: Longer flat walk or short climb; good path.
Grade 3: Moderately difficult walk or climb, over a long distance or involving some steep climbing; track may be rough in places.
Grade 4: Difficult, steep mountain climb or multi-day backpacking hike; some prior bushwalking experience is advisable.

These grades are a general guide only; consult the text for more details.

It is important to prepare well for these walks and always carry drinking water, food and warm clothing. Weather conditions can change rapidly in the South West, and the power of nature should always be respected. The possibilities for bush-walking are endless in this varied and spectacular part of Western Australia, and further information is available at local tourist bureaus.

OPPOSITE The scenic Willyabrup Cliffs, passed on the Cape to Cape Walk (see p. 143), are a popular place for abseiling and rock climbing.

The Bibbulmun Track: Grades 1–4 (depending on the distance walked)

The Bibbulmun (see map, page 10) is one of the longest continually marked tracks in Australia, extending from Kalamunda to Albany, a distance of 950 kilometres. Maps and guidebooks for the walk are available from the Department of Conservation and Land Management, bookstores and tourist bureaus. The track passes through the diverse and unique forests of the South West, descends into deep river valleys, climbs granite peaks and traverses cliff edges on the southern coast. Almost the entire distance passes through natural environments. The trail symbol is the Waugal, or rainbow serpent, a spirit being from the Aboriginal Dreamtime. Three-sided timber shelters are provided every 10–20 kilometres along the track, with rainwater tanks, bush toilets and, occasionally, fireplaces. The shelters are built away from roads to minimize vandalism and provide more of a wilderness experience. There is no charge for the use of any of the facilities. The Bibbulmun does pass through some of the towns of the South West including Dwellingup, Balingup, Pemberton, Northcliffe and Walpole, allowing hikers to replenish their food supplies. These towns offer alternative accommodation, with many bed-and-breakfasts, chalet complexes and guesthouses providing transport to and from the track, enabling you to sleep in comfort every night (if you prefer) while you walk a section of the track. At least 3–4 litres of water per person should be carried on the hike, and containers can be refilled every night at the shelters. There is no hiking register, so it is important to let someone 'at home' know your route and expected time of return. Many sections of the track can be completed as day or half-day walks, but if you want to walk the entire track it will probably take about six to eight weeks!

Walking the Bibbulmun Track is a unique way of exploring the South West, and I would certainly recommend wandering down at least a small section to gain an appreciation of our beautiful natural heritage. However, spending a week or more on the Bibbulmun is one of those experiences that could change your whole outlook on life. Either way, I hope you enjoy this wonderful track.

THE BUNBURY AND PEEL REGION

Murray River, Lane Poole Conservation Reserve: 9 kilometres, 4–5 hours, Grade 2

This is a walk along the lower Murray River from Nanga Road to Scarp Pool. The track (an old road) climbs over hills and through jarrah, marri and blackbutt forests above the valley, and then descends to the river itself, with its rapids and quiet pools. There are many wildflowers in spring and you can swim in some parts of the Murray in summer. The hike is not a circuit, so a car shuttle is required. The track ends at Scarp Pool, where it is necessary either to wade across the river (difficult in winter) or to use a flying fox, located about half a kilometre further downstream, to reach the car park. To find the flying fox, continue downstream along the track until you see a vague path leading down to the river just before the crossing of a small tributary stream.

Lake Pollard walk, Yalgorup National Park: 6 kilometres return, 2 hours, Grade 1

Lake Pollard is one of the salty lakes of the Yalgorup National Park. These lakes are very important breeding and habitat sites for many species of waterbird, including migratory waders from the northern hemisphere. The walk begins at the entrance to Martins Tank camping ground on Preston Beach Road and leads through tuart and banksia woodland to the lake and a bird hide. The track has interesting coastal plain vegetation communities and an abundance of bird life, including black swans that frequent the lake in the warmer months, from October to March.

Sika circuit, Wellington National Park: 9.4 kilometres, 4 hours, Grade 3

This is an excellent circuit walk in the central jarrah forest, starting from near the kiosk at Wellington Dam. It wends in a westerly direction from here along ridges thickly forested with jarrah and marri, and then descends to the Collie River, following its course upstream back to the dam. This walk has beautiful river and forest scenery, with small patches of huge old growth trees and a wide variety of vegetation. The Collie River has impressive rapids and inviting large pools in what appears to be a wilderness area. However, there is actually a road not too far away on the other side of the river (only noticed when a car drives along it) and I would advise against skinny-dipping!

THE SOUTH WEST CAPES

Cape to Cape Walk Track: Grades 1–4 (depending on the distance walked)

This is a 120 kilometre long walk between the scenic capes of Naturaliste and Leeuwin, with many sections suitable as half-day or full day outings. Pamphlets about the track are available from the Department of Conservation and Land Management or local tourist bureaus. Bush campsites with only minimal facilities are provided some distance from vehicle access points, and fuel stoves must be used (fires are prohibited). Adequate food and water should be carried (at least 3 litres of water per person per day), although stocks can be replenished at the small towns of Yallingup, Gracetown, Prevelly and Hamelin Bay, which are passed along the way. The Cape to Cape Walk is superb, traversing some of the best coastal scenery in Australia and some magnificent stretches of wild country.

Bunker Bay and lighthouse, Cape Naturaliste: 3.7 kilometres, 1.5–2 hours, Grade 2

This circuit walk begins at the Bunker Bay car park and winds through coastal heaths and woodlands to the Cape Naturaliste lighthouse, built in 1903 from local limestone. There are lookout points over the rugged coastline and Geographe Bay, where you might spot humpback or southern right whales between September and November. Although this track is rocky in places and has uphill and downhill sections, it has much to offer the walker, with excellent views and many wildflowers in springtime.

Wardanup trail, Yallingup: 5 kilometres, 2.5 hours, Grade 2

This circuit walk starts at the Rabbits car park at Yallingup town site and initially heads north along the coast before striking inland to ascend to the top of Wardanup Hill, at 173 metres above sea level. The path turns south from here to a lookout point and then descends past Ngilgi Cave to Caves House. From here, follow the 'Ghost Trail' (see page 74) along a collapsed limestone gorge back to Yallingup town site. The hike has an interesting mix of vegetation and excellent coastal views, and there is also the opportunity to visit Ngilgi Cave if you wish.

Meekadarribee Falls, 'Ellensbrook': 2 kilometres return, 40 minutes, Grade 1, wheelchair accessible

This is an enchanting short walk to a peppermint tree grotto, with a crystal-clear stream and small waterfall cascading over moss-covered limestone rocks. There is a small cave here, said to be haunted by the spirits of the Aboriginal lovers Mitanne and Nobel (see page 79). The walk is also interesting for its European heritage, as it starts from 'Ellensbrook' homestead, the first home of Alfred and Ellen Bussell, built in 1857 from crushed shell and limestone.

THE TALL FORESTS

Bridgetown Jarrah Park: Faller's Brand trail, 3.2 kilometres, 1 hour, Grade 1; Hollow Karri trail, 4.5 kilometres, 90 minutes, Grade 1

This park on the Brockman Highway between Nannup and Bridgetown was formed by a local community group, the Bridgetown-Greenbushes Friends of the Forest. There are a number of walk tracks here, wending their way through the beautiful and varied forest. Most of the park has been logged but this was many years ago, when harvesting was more selective. There are still the occasional enormous jarrah, marri, karri and blackbutt trees and a wide variety of understorey vegetation, with many wildflowers in springtime. The trails are generally flat, well marked and suitable for almost everyone.

Dave Evans Bicentennial Tree to Warren lookout, Warren National Park: 2.4 kilometres return, 1 hour, Grade 1

This is an excellent walk through awesome old growth karri forest. The wide and mostly flat path leads from the Dave Evans Bicentennial Tree to a lookout over the Warren River, past old giants of the forest, with their large burls, and vigorous younger karris growing wherever there is a gap in the canopy. The bird life is prolific: iridescent blue splendid fairy wrens, purple-crowned lorikeets and scarlet robins are all common species. There are picnic facilities and barbecues at the Bicentennial Tree, which can also be climbed if you are game!

Lane Poole Falls, Boorara National Park: 5 kilometres return, 2 hours, Grade 2

This is a delightful walk starting from the Boorara Tree and wending through karri and marri forest to the Lane Poole Falls on the Canterbury River. The falls are about 12 metres high and flow best in winter and spring. The walk meanders at first through older regrowth forest and then descends steeply into a valley filled with giant karri trees. The wildflowers on this walk are spectacular in springtime, with the red, white and purple of coral vine, clematis and tree hovea creating vibrant splashes of colour among the towering smooth-barked karris.

Northcliffe Forest Park: Twin Karri Loop, 400 metres, 20 minutes, Grade 1; Marri Meander, 3.5 kilometres, 1.5–2 hours, Grade 2

Northcliffe Forest Park, managed by the Northcliffe community, is an area of relatively undisturbed karri and marri forest. Both of these walks start from the Hollow Butt picnic area, named for a giant karri tree that has been hollowed out over the ages by fires. The tracks here pass through thick undergrowth and are relatively rough walking, but there are many beautiful giant trees, and the forest has an abundance of bird life.

Quinninup Forest walks: King Karri Walk, 4.2 kilometres, 2 hours, Grade 2; Ridgeback Walk, 5 kilometres, 3 hours, Grade 2

The Quinninup Forest walks have been created by the Quinninup Community Association in association with the Living Windows program, and feature old growth karri and jarrah forest, with their diverse and rich understorey plant life. The King Karri Walk has many giant karri trees, while the Ridgeback Walk is a more challenging, hilly walk through jarrah and karri forest. These two walks are illustrated in detail in a gazebo at the corner of Wheatley Coast and Junction roads, Quinninup.

OPPOSITE TOP The beautiful Lane Poole Falls are reached after a very pleasant walk through karri forest in the Boorara Conservation Park.
OPPOSITE BOTTOM Misty early morning at one of the Bibbulmun Track huts near the Murray River, Lane Poole Conservation Reserve.

Mt Chudalup, D'Entrecasteaux National Park: 1 kilometre return, 30 minutes, Grade 2

Mt Chudalup is an excellent short climb, with an interesting mix of vegetation, and boasts sweeping views from the summit over the heath-covered plains to the south coast. The walk starts off among large karri and marri trees and then climbs through granite herb fields and pockets of bullich and *Xanthorrhoea* grass trees to the 188 metre high peak. The last section is up a bare granite slope and is moderately steep. The hiker is rewarded with sweeping vistas of the D'Entrecasteaux National Park from the large summit dome.

PREVIOUS SPREAD Bates Peak from the summit of Devils Slide, Porongurup Range.
BELOW The first part of the Great Forest Trees Walk, in the Shannon National Park, passes through an impressive old growth forest, with karri, jarrah and marri all present.

Mokares Rock and Shannon Dam, Shannon National Park: 5.5 kilometres, 2 hours, Grade 2

Mokares Rock is an interesting circuit walk beginning at the Shannon picnic area just off the South Western Highway. The walk is mainly through regrowth forest, but there is a wide variety of vegetation and forest types. The track starts through karri trees to Smeathers Rock and then climbs steadily up to Mokares Rock through jarrah and marri dominated forest. There are good views from here across the Shannon Basin. The walk descends again to the picturesque Shannon Dam and follows the river back to the picnic area. There is a quokka hide near the start of the walk, situated in dense riverine vegetation favoured by these shy marsupials (mainland quokkas are far less outgoing than their Rottnest cousins). They can sometimes be seen at dawn foraging through the undergrowth.

Great Forest Trees Walk, Shannon National Park: 8 kilometres return, 3 hours, Grade 2

This is an excellent forest walk connecting the northern one-way arms of the Great Forest Trees Drive. The walk is not a circuit, and so it is possible to do a 4 kilometre one-way walk if you have a car shuttle. The hike starts in beautiful old growth forest, with jarrah, marri and karri all present, and wends down to a footbridge over the Shannon River, which generally flows only in winter and spring. From here, the track has some moderately steep sections as it climbs out of the valley through mixed forest areas to meet up again with the drive. Even if you do not intend doing the whole walk, I would recommend strolling down to the Shannon River and back, through the magnificent old trees with their teeming bird life.

Climbing Mt Frankland in the Great Southern region.

Mt Frankland: 2 kilometres return, 1–2 hours, Grade 2

The Mt Frankland National Park is a stunning wilderness area with some of the most beautiful forest and hills scenery in the South West. It offers outstanding backpack hiking for experienced bush-walkers to places like Mt Roe. Mt Frankland itself has an excellent short climb to its 422 metre high peak. The track is steep in places but easy to follow, with concrete steps and a short metal ladder to aid in the ascent. The summit offers 360 degree views over seemingly endless forests. The feeling of solitude and wilderness is marred only by the operational fire-spotting tower situated on top of the peak. You can descend the way you came or by an alternative path that circumnavigates the mountain, eventually leading back to the camping area. This is a short distance further but is highly recommended, as it passes through majestic karri forest and over moss and lichen covered rocks, with spectacular wild-flowers in spring and early summer.

Nuyts Wilderness Walk, Walpole-Nornalup National Park: 15 kilometres return, 6–8 hours, Grade 3

Part of the western section of the Walpole-Nornalup National Park is known as the Nuyts Wilderness Area and is not accessible to vehicles of any kind. This area is a bushwalking paradise. There is a long track from Shedley Drive to the south coast, where hikers can discover the beautiful Thompson or Aldridge coves near Point Nuyts. Thompson Cove has a wonderful camping area nestled in a grove of peppermint trees, for a night or two away from it all in the wilderness. The walk has an interesting range of vegetation, with tall karri forest, marri and banksia woodland and coastal heaths and sand dunes.

Mt Lindesay: 8 kilometres return, 3–4 hours, Grade 3

Mt Lindesay, at 445 metres, is the highest peak in the Denmark district. A gravel road heads 22 kilometres north from Denmark to a picnic site on the Denmark River at the base of the hill. The river has small rapids and is overhung by large jarrah and marri trees. From here, it is a long and challenging climb through forest, rocky slopes and heathland to the broad summit plateau. There are good views on the way up and some excellent wildflowers in spring and early summer. Mt Frankland can be seen way over in the west, and you might be able to see the Stirling and Porongurup ranges to the north-east on a clear day.

West Cape Howe: 7 kilometres return, 3 hours, Grade 2

West Cape Howe is only accessible by four-wheel-drive vehicle or by old-fashioned walking. The path starts from Shelley Beach in West Cape Howe National Park, climbing up and around a deep valley in the limestone hills, and then follows vehicle tracks part of the way to the awesome cliffs of West Cape Howe. The scenery here is unique, with jet black dolerite rocks, giant chasms and superb white beaches. It is essential to carry warm clothing on this hike, as the wind chill factor can be extreme, with only the Southern Ocean between these cliffs and Antarctica!

Torndirrup National Park:

- **Peak Head, 5 kilometres, 2–3 hours return, Grade 2:** This is a good walk to a prominent granite headland that is popular with experienced rock climbers.
- **Point Possession Heritage Trail, 4 kilometres, 2 hours return, Grade 2:** The heritage trail provides a varied and interesting walk passing over a sandy isthmus joining Point Possession and the Vancouver Peninsula. The Englishman George Vancouver made his historic landing here in 1791. The trail passes initially through coastal heathlands with patches of low jarrah/marri forest and then traverses the beaches and granite rocks of the headland.
- **Bald Head, 16 kilometres, 6–8 hours return, Grade 3:** This is an outstanding bushwalk along Flinders Peninsula to Limestone Head and Bald Head, with varied vegetation and geology and stunning coastal scenery. The hike is long, involving a lot of uphill and downhill walking, and there is no water available along the route.

Porongurup National Park:

- **Wansborough walk, 3 kilometres one way (from the Tree-in-the-Rock picnic area to Mira Flores Road), 1–2 hours, Grade 1:** This is a gentle climb over one of the passes in the range, with beautiful karri forest and many wildflowers in springtime. Most people ascend to the highest point of the pass and then return to the Tree-in-the-Rock picnic area, a distance of 4 kilometres return.
- **Nancy and Hayward peak circuit, 5 kilometres, 2–3 hours, Grade 2:** This is an excellent walk along the crest of the range, with fine views south

towards Albany and north to the Stirling Range. There is a wide variety of vegetation, from dense karri and marri forest to granite moss and herb gardens.

- **Devils Slide, 4 kilometres return, 2–3 hours, Grade 3:** This walk up to the highest point in the Porongurup Range is reasonably steep in places but offers panoramic views.
- **Castle Rock, 3 kilometres return, 1.5–2 hours, Grade 2:** This is a short walk to a prominent granite outcrop and the amazing Balancing Rock. The final ascent requires some gymnastics!

Stirling Range National Park:

- **Bluff Knoll, 6 kilometres return, 3–4 hours, Grade 3:** This is a long, moderately steep climb up to the highest point in the southern half of Western Australia, with a good path and magnificent wildflowers from August to December.
- **Toolbrunup, 4 kilometres return, 3–4 hours, Grade 4:** Toolbrunup is a far more difficult climb than Bluff Knoll, with rocky, steep and exposed sections. The summit has an amazing 360 degree view—arguably the best in the Stirling Range.
- **Warrungup (Mt Trio), 3 kilometres return, 2–3 hours, Grade 3:** This is a moderately steep climb, with interesting rock formations and excellent wildflowers in springtime, including the common mountain bell (*Darwinia lejostyla*), hakeas, dryandras and *Nemcia* peas.
- **Baby Barnett Hill, 1.5 kilometres return, 1 hour, Grade 2:** On this short, relatively easy climb there are good wildflowers in spring, including the beautiful Mondurup bell (*Darwinia macrostegia*).

- **Mt Hassell, 3 kilometres return, 2–3 hours, Grade 3:** A moderate climb up to the conical rocky summit will reward you with views of Toolbrunup and the western Stirling Range.
- **Talyuberlup, 3 kilometres return, 2–3 hours, Grade 3:** This short, steep climb offers excellent views from the summit. The peak has numerous rock pillars, caves and pinnacles like the ruins of a gigantic medieval castle and is fascinating to explore.
- **Stirling Ridge Walk, about 20 kilometres (but it feels much longer!), Grade 4+:** This is one of the hardest and best bushwalks available in the South West, with rugged terrain and excruciatingly dense bush but amazing mountain scenery. The complete walk from Bluff Knoll to Ellen Peak requires a car shuttle and takes two to three days; alternatively, you can ascend the First Arrow, traverse to Ellen Peak and then descend to the plains. This alternative hike, known as the Arrows Circuit, takes two days, with no shuttle required. Walkers should be experienced and need to carry at least 3 litres of water per person per day, as there are no reliable water sources on the ridge. Nights are usually spent in small caves in the mountains or in limited areas suitable for bush camping.

For more information on the Stirling and Porongurup ranges, and full descriptions of the bushwalks available there, see *Dawn till Dusk in the Stirling and Porongurup Ranges* by Rob and Stuart Olver, University of Western Australia Press, 1998.

SELECT REFERENCES

Cross, J., ed., *Journal of Several Expeditions Made in W.A. during the Years 1829, 30, 31, 32*, facsimile edn, University of Western Australia Press, Nedlands, 1980.

Department of Conservation and Land Management, *Bushwalks in the South West*, Perth, 1997.

Green, N., *Broken Spears: Aborigines and Europeans in the Southwest of Australia*, Focus Education Services, Cottesloe, 1984.

Haebich, A., *For their Own Good: Aborigines and Government in the South West of Western Australia, 1900–1940*, 2nd edn, University of Western Australia Press, Nedlands, 1992.

Kelly, P. C., *Western Australian Year Book 1997*, Australian Bureau of Statistics, Perth, 1997.

Lockyer, E., 'Journal of Major Lockyer: Commandant [sic] of the Expedition Sent from Sydney in 1826 to Found a Settlement at King George's Sound, Western Australia', 1826, copy held in Battye Library.

Meney, K., *Forests on Foot: 40 Walks in the Forests of the South West of Western Australia*, Campaign to Save Native Forests, South Perth, 1985.

Murray Districts Aboriginal Association, *The Pinjarra Massacre*, pamphlet, Pinjarra, 1998.

Seddon, G., *Sense of Place*, University of Western Australia Press, Nedlands, 1972.

Sellick, D., *First Impressions Albany 1791–1801: Traveller's Tales*, Western Australian Museum, Perth, 1997.